Planning a Party

A Step by Step Guide from Start to Finish & Beyond Fun

(A Guide to Planning Great Parties and Great Ideas to Get a Successful Party Event)

Nicolas Davis

Published By **Oliver Leish**

Nicolas Davis

All Rights Reserved

Planning a Party: A Step by Step Guide from Start to Finish & Beyond Fun (A Guide to Planning Great Parties and Great Ideas to Get a Successful Party Event)

ISBN 978-1-7752436-9-4

No part of this guidebook shall be reproduced in any form without permission in writing from the publisher except in the case of brief quotations embodied in critical articles or reviews.

Legal & Disclaimer

The information contained in this book is not designed to replace or take the place of any form of medicine or professional medical advice. The information in this book has been provided for educational & entertainment purposes only.

The information contained in this book has been compiled from sources deemed reliable, and it is accurate to the best of the Author's knowledge; however, the Author cannot guarantee its accuracy and validity and cannot be held liable for any errors or omissions. Changes are periodically made to this book. You must consult your doctor or get professional medical advice before using any of the suggested remedies, techniques, or information in this book.

Upon using the information contained in this book, you agree to hold harmless the Author from and against any damages, costs, and expenses, including any legal fees potentially resulting from the application of any of the information provided by this guide. This disclaimer applies to any damages or injury caused by the use and application, whether directly or indirectly, of any advice or information presented, whether for breach of contract, tort, negligence, personal injury, criminal intent, or under any other cause of action.

You agree to accept all risks of using the information presented inside this book. You need to consult a professional medical practitioner in order to ensure you are both able and healthy enough to participate in this program.

Table Of Contents

Chapter 1: How To Schedule Your Party Preparations 1

Chapter 2: Will Your Event Have A Style? 11

Chapter 3: Tips For Celebration Rentals . 25

Chapter 4: The Best Ways To Arrange Your Celebration Preparations 43

Chapter 5: Tips For Developing A Perfect Seats Prepare For Your Event 57

Chapter 6: Importance Behind The Planning 72

Chapter 7: Learning The Basics 75

Chapter 8: Choosing The Perfect Theme 79

Chapter 9: Begin Preparations 82

Chapter 10: Midway Through The Prep . 86

Chapter 11: Review & Revise Plan (If Necessary) 89

Chapter 12: Finalize The Plan 92

Chapter 13: Party Time! 95

Chapter 14: The Party's Over 98

Chapter 15: For No Reason At All 100

Chapter 16: Theme Ideas 103

Chapter 17: Choosing The Type Of Party 111

Chapter 18: Picking Up Eatables 118

Chapter 19: Rearranging Furniture 125

Chapter 20: Make It Collaborative 131

Chapter 21: How To Scent The Air For A Party 136

Chapter 22: The Mistakes To Avoid 141

Chapter 23: Preparing Cocktails 146

Chapter 24: Easy Clean Up After The Party 152

Chapter 25: Party Ideas 155

Chapter 26: Games 166

Chapter 1: How To Schedule Your Party Preparations

If you plan your event early enough You will not only reduce stress, however you could also make savings. Many people organize their events in the early months of each year by contemplating holiday celebrations, birthdays, or other celebrations. If you're the type that hosts a large number of events, this is an perfect time to begin planning your celebrations since you are able to shop for your essential party items during the entire year and get deals as you come across these items. If you have a clear idea of what date you'll hold your first gathering, then you are able to start planning the party.

First, choose the day and then choose the theme (if you're planning to choose one). Your theme will dictate a lot on the details of your event. Choose the venue. If it is at your house, then it will save you the cost of renting an event location. If you're going to an outside location You will have verify the availability of the venue and reserve the venue. Next, you will need to determine the budget. Make a budget plan that lists all costs for the event, including invitations as well as decorations, food drinks, entertainment as well as rental expenses and personnel hiring (if there is any). You should also decide whether you wish to engage the assistance of an event coordinator.

When the venue, date and budget have been set, it is time to begin the planning. If you plan to hire any equipment make sure you book it as soon as is possible. Do not leave it until two weeks prior to the event or you could discover that the equipment you are looking for has already been booked. This is the same for whatever entertainment you wish to book. Many entertainers have bookings months ahead, so prepare yourself to book before the deadline or you will miss out.

Invitations need to be designed to be written, printed and distributed. It is important to ensure that you have the RVSP time is well noted as well as it allows ample time to prepare to the amount of people attending. Begin thinking about menu suggestions and decor early to be able to purchase the things as you come across these items, either at a discount or in stock. The most popular holidays like Halloween and Christmas have plenty of costumes and decorations available before the start of the season. If you are able to buy them in time, the budget you have set may be much less strained.

When the RSVP day has come and gone then count up the guests who will be attending and prepare your menu to serve at the event. If you're providing snacks, with no or no effort, these are able to be purchased beforehand. If you're preparing your party's food, think about what recipes you can prepare and frozen prior to the party. This can help you free your time for the day of the event.

Contact the rental provider at least a few days before the event to confirm the delivery date and make sure you are able in assembling any equipment. Be sure that your outfit is in order and that you have ample time before the celebration to make sure you are prepared for the party. If you've done your homework and are well-prepared, you'll be as happy as the guests!

WHAT TYPE OF CELEBRATION WILL YOU HOST?

The possibilities for the type of event you can organize are endless. When you decide on the type of celebration you're planning to hold is the first step in determining the way you will prepare for your event. A few points to think about while selecting the kind of event you'll be hosting:

Are you planning an event specifically for someone specific for a specific person, like an anniversary celebration, graduation celebrations at college, wedding or even a welcome house party? There is a need to look into their accessibility and preferences, and also whether they'd like to be invited to the celebration. If you're planning to throw a sour surprise for someone surely you'll need to decide on these options without contacting the person in question.

1. Celebrations for Gives and other events are usually attended by people who are similar to you, so keep this in mind when planning your event.

It is fun to host, but will require some preparatory work. If you are planning to take the long distances required in order to get to the party, it is important to consider your timetable for the event.

2. Costume-themed events like Halloween or Costume celebrations are great to

organize. Be sure to let your guests to know exactly what they need for them with regards to dress and dress code.

Dinner events may differ. What about an event for a meal in which guests are a part of the food? If you plan to throw a gathering that will serve the guests a dinner or some other type of food, be sure that you are aware of your guests' number and budget for food preparation as well as beverages.

What kind of event that you throw will be a lot dependent on your. If you're a novice to planning a party, choose simple events. If you enjoy throwing big and themed parties after that go for it!

JUST HOW MUCH WILL YOUR CELEBRATION EXPENSE?

If you make a budget schedule prior to buying the necessary items for your event You will know beforehand what it's going to cost. Great events don't have to cost a lot of money. If you plan ahead and are able to plan it and have the time, you can put together great events on the budget of a small amount.

Begin by drawing up an arrangement of everything you're likely to need for the celebration. The initial column needs comprise the next with items:

1. Sending invitations as well as mailing expenses

2. Location hiring (otherwise in competition with the house).

3. Equipment employ (have a distinct malfunction of the same for each device).

4. Designs.

5. Food.

6. Home entertainment.

7. The team (wedding food, catering or other set-up personnel as required).

The 2nd column should include a budget plan price estimate, and additionally on each over item, a minimum and the maximum amount of money you are willing to put into the item.

If the bigger event you're planning and the more formal your event, you'll most likely discover many more organizations spending money. The wedding budget organizer will become a great deal bigger since it'll need items like flowers and match-leasing and wedding gowns transport, and more.

If you're planning to utilize an event organizer, making a budget plan before you meet with them is an excellent suggestion. Your budget will serve as a guideline for your demands and requirements. The party organizer will definitely then know precisely the things you can and cannot handle.

Keep in mind that spending large sums of money will result in a less successful occasion. It is possible to save money through a creative approach and also deciding which areas are best spent. Here are some suggestions to minimize the impact of your occasion:.

1. Create or design on your computer personal invitations, in addition to hand-deliver an email if possible.

Make them inflate on your own using a hired out Helium storage tank. Cutting flowers and plants from your backyard can be a great addition to the design of any.

3. You can host the party at your own home, if you have enough.

4. Take the time to cook your own food, or host the event during the middle of the day when the large meal is not planned.

5. Take chairs and tables from friends. Ask them for their assistance in establishing and then offer to set up exactly the same thing to them if they are having an event.

6. Assist teens in providing fun for birthday celebrations of children. activities.

Planning your budget well will be efficient and you'll not be able to finance a costly celebration!

If you develop a budget strategy prior to buying items for your celebration, you'll be able to see in the development the amount it'll cost you.

Does the celebration take place for one particular person like an anniversary celebration, wedding, graduation ceremony or a welcome home celebration? If people are making an extended journey for the occasion, it is important to consider the time of your celebration. Events that are themed like Halloween and Fancy Dress-up events are great to host.

Chapter 2: Will Your Event Have A Style?

If you're throwing the 4th of July celebration or Halloween-themed party You can add many props that will help create the atmosphere. If your Halloween event is a dress-up one the guests be faced with get the appropriate attire.

These celebrations can be fun but they can also make people feel uneasy. If you're hosting the theme of your party, think about the people you would like to invite and ask them whether they are willing to be part of the party and also really dress it things up. In the event that they do not, keep your theme as simple or adaptable in order to let them decide to be involved, or not.

If you're planning to set up the atmosphere using a particular theme However, make it simple for guests to get in the mood Think about something easy like a party with a hat or an event with a theme of color. People can choose what exactly they agree in with, dependant on the extent to which they plan to integrate themselves into the atmosphere of the event.

Themed parties can also consist of crafting celebrations. Craft events are a great option to celebrate children's birthdays, and to social teams that have close knits.

In the event of throwing an theme party and you aren't able to decide what items to make use of and the way you'll decorate to the occasion You might want to incorporate the look in your menu. You could also throw the typical afternoon party, that you provide your guests with cups of tea served in china and also serve cucumber sandwiches, as well as Butterfly pies to enjoy.

These kinds of celebrations can be fun to plan and pleasant for visitors when they truly feel a part of the event. The events won't be suitable ideal for everyone but are definitely worth an attempt if you, as the host, are a fan of these kinds of events.

THAT WILL YOU WELCOME TO THE EVENT?

If you are hosting a party dedicated to a specific person, then you need to know who they'd love to be welcomed at the party. If the event is something that's official, like the wedding or Bar Mitzvah there are certain people who must be greeted and the list of guests should be kept on in the list of guests. Inadvertently bringing Great-aunt Edna to your child's baptism ceremony could cause many tensions among the household, which that you'll want to avoid.

If you're planning to throw an Independence Day or Halloween party, you can decorate your space using numerous props that will help create the setting. If you are throwing a party that is style-oriented in addition to deciding precisely the type of event you'll create and how you'll decorate to the occasion You may want to incorporate the design in your menu selection. A themed celebration could also comprise of craft events. If you are hosting a party dedicated to a specific person then you'll have to consider who they'd prefer to attend the event. If the event is a private event for instance, a small dinner party, then you'll have to decide the people that you wish to include by observing the way they interact.

If you're throwing an unexpected surprise to a loved one, you may be required to discuss with friends who might want to join in the celebration. It is essential that someone will be as the official guest to the party each time following everyone else has arrived, so that the surprise is sure to be memorable.

A guest's list could be the top things to take into consideration when planning your event. A party should be fun and enjoyable. Visitors who are the best will ensure that this happens.

If you're planning an event specifically for teenagers it is essential to think about in the amount of people who will attend, the chance that some guests might be trying to get banned substances, and the many grown-ups will need to supervise. If the majority of them aren't included on the list then they aren't allowed to attend the occasion.

The best people can definitely make your occasion a huge event that is a success. If you invite the wrong people, it can turn your carefully planned occasion into a disaster.

If your celebration is intimate for instance, a dinner occasion, you'll have to decide who you would like to invite by the way they interact. It is possible to organize two separate dinner parties to keep them all interested! If you're hosting dinner parties for your colleagues from the company, take note of the strengths and weaknesses that the group has.

WHAT IS YOUR EVENT GOWN CODE?

The dress code for your event will be a vital decision you'll make during the preparations for your event. Imagine going to an event with mixed drinks wearing tracksuit pants, this individual would definitely regret it in the event they weren't aware about the dress code like everyone did.

Kinds of Outfit Codes:

1. Laid-back is a popular choice to be worn at a lot of events, specifically backyard barbecues and unexpected events. People can wear whatever they want, however it's best to avoid wearing a sloppy manner!

2. Formal Dress as over but slightly better. Take off your trousers, shirts and shorts.

3. Evening/Cocktail generally a small dress in black or a short fashionable dress suitable for women with men who are compatible, whether or not there is a connection.

4. The Black Tie/Formal Guy should wear an elegant coat. For ladies this could mean a cocktail look or long dress which is elegant enough.

5. White Connection is a formal attire. Females should wear a long gowns and, for men, the white connection coat as well as a vest, and t-shirt.

6. After Five or Semi-Formal is not as official in the same way as Black Connection, just like mixed drink clothing which is typically seen on invitations to wedding receptions.

7. Black Connection Optional You could wear a coat or long gown and it will be formal. However, if it is mentioned on the invitation men can choose the dark color and connections instead, while women could dress more casually. It is up to the person attending.

Joyful Dress This type of outfit is usually connected to a theme celebration. If it's an

Xmas celebration, she could wear a fiery mix drink red dress as well as sparkling jewelry.

9. Costumed celebrations Make it explicit on the invitation the subject matter to let guests know the attire they are expected to wear. There is a possibility of having an Shade theme as well as the theme of a Costume theme or an Swimming pool Event motif or an event Occasion design (such such as Halloween).

There is no need to insist on a dress code. Instead, you can let guests to dress with whatever outfit they are most comfortable in. If you don't want certain guests to be dressed in denims or other alcoholic dress gowns, be sure to make that explicit on your invitation in establishing the dress codes for the event.

CONCEPTS FOR EVENT DECORATIONS

There are a lot of different kinds of celebrations that you can host, and therefore there is an endless number of ideas of decorations for your event. If the event has an theme, the decorations are sure to help set the mood as well as enhance how the party is planned.

Fourth of July decorations with white, red and blue by making use of banners, balloons and even balloons. Add a splash of celebrity fireworks and attach the chairs with patriotic bows.

Set up posters with famous songs from the 50s. Create notes on songs from the black cardstock and hang them over the walls.

Pool Party You may like to choose an exotic theme to your pool party decoration. Your guests should be greeted with flowers. Play 50s browse songs.

Kids' Events: You can choose to use balloons, plates with matching papers and napkins made of paper as well as banners for every type of birthday party for kids However, if the child chooses a theme then you must decorate it appropriately. Events for pirates require swords as well as ships. The fairy-themed celebrations require wings, sticks and glamorous celebrities.

Use your creative flair as your source of inspiration to decorate the event. The event doesn't have to cost much, simply create something new and enjoy fun!

Valentines Day Hearts as well as blooms make up the primary decoration for this particular celebration. Set the mood by lighting lots of candles lighting. Begin by welcoming all women guests by presenting them with a rose.

Sports activity celebration If you're planning the ball to mark the group's success or participation at the top of the table, it is possible to enhance the event by incorporating the colors of your organization. If you are playing football or other sporting events in the region, make the table make it appear as a party place with a few objective objects in each corner.

SUGGESTIONS FOR EVENT AMUSEMENT

Selecting what kind of music is contingent on the type of celebration and also the guests who will be attending. If you are planning a themed event, look at the following suggestions for music entertainment:

1. Jukeboxes for 50s and 60s-themed occasions or for Sock Jumps

2. Karaoke device for sing along events

3. The 70s party songs from Nightclub

4. Music for swimming pool and beach celebrations

5. Irish music for St Patrick's Day events

Other home entertainment ideas could include:

1. Behind-the-scenes films playing for festive atmosphere. For an Oscar event, it is possible to include older Oscar winners

playing as well as a themed party for the eighties is sure to have motion-pictures taken from the eighties having a blast.

2. The use of a handheld viewer to allow guests to keep their plethora of dollars surveyed would surely help with Halloween festivities and spark conversation in workplace parties.

3. The road illusionist may circle between the juggling techniques of visitors according to the need.

Gaming can be integrated in the design of your event. The Gambling Enterprise Night includes tables, roulette as well as any other games that are video-based however, you can also incorporate video games into other events. Limbo is a popular game. Limbo is an absolute favorite for any event that includes music!

If the event takes place outside, there is the possibility to organize sporting events like beach balls communication, sack race, and group passes the orange. They're great to get guests to get together and to unwind.

Concepts for a fun event for children:

1. Engage with a clown or an illusionist to have fun

2. The pass-the-parcel, the music chairs, putting the tail on a donkey, and so on are classic party favorites and are sure to keep the kids engaged.

They are great for enthralling young children, and you are sure to have something they can remember that they've done. It is possible to collaborate with an expert for this job.

4. The Witch Hunt game is another popular. Kids love this type of game since they do not know what kind of reward they might find.

Your dress code for the event will be an important decision you take in the planning process for your party. Celebrations themed to the theme Make explicit on the invite what the theme will be to let guests know what attire is expected. If the event has a design, the patterns will assist in establishing the frame of mind as well as add the overall theme of the event. A sporting event, if you're planning to throw an event in celebration of your team's having won or making it to the finals then you can decorate the celebration space with the colors of the group. A Swimming Pool Celebration want to create extravagant style to the pool party designs.

Ideas for entertainment at home to entertain guests are numerous, but don't get disengaged from having the best entertainment options. People do not always need to entertain themselves, many prefer to take a break while they chat or just dance. Remember that people often create their own fun.

Chapter 3: Tips For Celebration Rentals

What exactly do you need to lease for your celebration? There are a lot of things to consider before deciding to lease equipment for your event. Here are some ideas to consider when deciding if you need to rent your party equipment:

What is the number of people attending your event? If you're not getting the bonus then you definitely need to think about hiring this tool.

Look at your event budget plan. It would certainly be cheaper to rent an area where everything that you need are provided?

3. If you decide to surely be leasing, you should have an inventory of each requirement you'll require, as well as all of the information about the celebration (budget schedule, guest numbers or days, times the theme, dress code) before you find an event-related rental service.

4. Don't limit the renting of your information to just two weeks before your event or you may be disappointed. Make contact with them in advance of the time (a minimum of one month) to determine whether all the information you require is available.

5. Find a rental shop for events which has a specialist for events that you could discuss your demands with.

6. When you've completed the payment for all items you need to rent out, be sure to pay careful attention to the lease. Find out exactly what you're legally responsible for when it comes costs for issues with the equipment.

7. Get a written failure of the cost of every item you rent out.

Check the issue of all the devices you're leasing before signing the contract. Be sure that every thing is working properly.

The time of your arrival, the timing of pickup at the end of the party and the event if you'll require help in setting up. There is a possibility of utilizing some reliable companions to assist you with this, but when you've used professional equipment and equipment, an expert set-up staff may be necessary.

10. When the time is over, check everything was rented to you and take note for any problems. Prepare to pay to cover this, based on the arrangement.

The rental of party equipment can make a lot of stress off of planning your party. Just make sure that you've given it to someone and you have enough assistance when putting together and also removing the tools any tension to keep the stress to an absolute minimal.

FOR HOW LONG SHOULD THE EVENT LAST?

Certain events need a certain date and time for the event, while others don't. Events that don't require the use of a space include:

1. Evening time activities

2. Events

3. Dancing and dancing events

Events that require duration of time include:

1. The celebrations are held in a place with a time limit. time

2. Birthday celebrations of the child

3. Mixer

Dance parties and parties could continue until the in the wee hours of morning. The hosts, need to determine the timing of your actions at the party even if the time for the cover wasn't stated in the invitation.

The wedding celebrations can last for more than 5 hours, if the wedding will be held at afternoon and the ceremony is adhered to. If you're holding the event at your private residence, the majority guests will definitely want to depart when the bride-to be and the groom have gone from the event.

Mixer events should run for around 2 hours. They usually take place in the days prior to events such as shows or the theater. It's a good idea to set the time of your event to give attendees to be able to arrive at the event after-cocktail.

Arrival time, timing of pickup following the event and the time you'll need help in setting-up. Some events need a particular duration for coatings, whereas other aren't. As the organizer, must establish the timing limit by your events at the party even if a time for the coating wasn't mentioned in the invitation. The wedding celebrations can be extended to over five hours, if the wedding ceremony is scheduled for afternoon and the wedding adheres to. Children's parties require an appropriate time for wrapping up especially the younger youngsters.

Children's parties need a time limit and a time limit, especially the young children. The older kids might prefer the event to last between 3 and as much as 4 hours. Sleeper party parties should be scheduled before lunch on the next day.

Being the host, it is on you to decide the appropriate time for your party. Choose it in accordance with your needs and demands of the event.

CREATIVE EVENT INVITE CONCEPTS

If you've decided on an event theme then you can get creative in your invitations. An impressive invitation will make your guests excited about what's coming.

1. What exactly the event was intended for (e.g. Infant shower, Shock 50th for Mark, Valentines Day celebration, Quilting event etc).

2. Day of day of the celebration.

3. Time of beginning (and and also covering) time.

4. The address of the event.

5. RSVP day.

6. The host's phone number for call calls.

7. Motif (if you have one).).

8. Gown Code.

It is possible to purchase themed invite cards, but you may prefer to use your own imagination. Computer system software which can assist you in creating cards. You can also create yourself.

1. If it's a typical celebration (such such as Xmas or Halloween, the Fourth of July, and St Patrick's Day) begin by choosing a color that represents the associated with the party. It is possible to pick an appropriate permit for St Patrick's Day or red or white, as well as blue to celebrate the Fourth of July.

Add embellishments to your card with the theme you choose. It is possible to add bows, or a tinted shine that matches the color of your choice.

If you are planning a dinosaur-themed event, it is possible to use an foot print template or even a bone. What is the best way to make making a snowman to be used for wintertime celebration? Shamrocks and hearts shapes are very easy to construct.

2. Choose a memorable slogan for your party. If you plan to have an event that is a Hat themed celebration you could have an are you are a Mad Hatter, or a show off event you might utilize a familiar calling card like Goal!

Food you serve will depend upon the day and time for the occasion. Events that are held during the middle of the day are most practical because they don't require much food. Here are some easy dishes to serve at parties:.

Simple Event Food Selection Concepts for Catering.

There are endless ideas for creative invitations to events. Make sure you create some amazing invitations.

What is the best way to find an eye spot to watch an event that is pirate-themed or small amount of fairy dirt (shine) to make the fairy-tale event? for the Oscar Evening or Golden World celebration, you can get a custom pet dog identification tag to gain entry. What is better than a betting ticket for the Kentucky Derby celebration?

1. Junk foods that are easy to cook include biscuits, cheese and snacks like nuts and chips. They also have crowns, chips, and dips. It is possible to buy dips, or prepare them by yourself.

If you've chosen the theme for your celebration and you're looking for a theme, then be creative with your invitations. If you have an event with a Hat themed celebration you may want to include a Do you an adolescent or for a flamboyant occasion, you may want to consider an old-fashioned showing off phone for example Goal!

The selection of foods you prefer depends on your preferences. Make sure it is in line with your personal style.

Fondue parties are fun and also easy to host. They were popular in the 1970s but they are back with the new century. You definitely need some fondues, and even greater than one superior, and you will be able to prepare different foods.

How do you make the eye-catching spot of the pirates or even a small fairy dust (shine) to make an event with a fairy theme? They can also be purchased to create their personal as part of your celebration's fun. Tea parties for midday can be easy to prepare various varieties of sandwiches and also having various varieties of desserts to enjoy together with tea as well as coffee.

Pizza, regardless of whether you buy takeaway or cook it yourself it is an essential meal that many consumers love. They can also be purchased to create your individual pizzas as part of an evening's home entertainment.

The mid-day tea party can be very straightforward to prepare diverse kinds of sandwiches. you can also choose from a variety of options of pie to serve along with tea and coffee. Delicious and delicious muffins are easy to prepare and can make a fantastic addition for any afternoon tea meal.

Prepare the potatoes to bake in their skins, then invite guests to fill them and garnish the dish with an assortment of decorations. This could consist of cheese, salsa, prepared onions, mushrooms chili beef, blueberry, olives, sour-lotion and tomatoes and hot sauces.

The bar-b-que concept suggests that someone needs prepared food while visitors will be there. BBQs can be made with various meats, like burgers, steak Kebobs, kebobs, and even food items that are seasoned like chicks. Kebobs, shrimp, and drumsticks are easy to consume in a standing position and are also more efficient to serve for more informal celebrations.

Pot dinners for good luck are a great idea because everyone brings food. Easy!

TIPS FOR PICKING DRINKS FOR THE CELEBRATION

For kids' events there isn't an issue to think about. If you are hosting an event that are sure to serve alcohol there are a myriad of types of drinks to fit the design of your celebration or even create an Bring Your Own (Bring Your Own) celebration.

Sparkling wine Strawberry Drink with alcohol

3 strawberries

and mug of pure topping sugar

1/3 mug Grand Marnier

2 tbsps lemon juice

Include all active ingredients, as well as the percentage of area on the bottom of the bubbly wine groove. Place sparkling wine on over the top.

In planning your drinks to be served at the kids' party make sure you don't rely on soft beverages. The event can be enhanced by adding theme and atmosphere of the event with the manner in which you provide your drinks. If you're hosting the event of a Tea Celebration for kids, provide them with china mugs and plates.

There is a good chance that you can provide several alcohol-based and non-alcoholic strike to your guests during the party. You can make your strike fun by serving them in a variety of bowls, and having multiple-shaped ice cubes floating in the bowls.

Trying to figure out how much alcohol you will serve for your gathering could prove hard. You may want to plan your catering in advance so you will not have to go out. Keep in mind that you must stick to your budget.

If you're serving draft beers as well as wine, you should have a couple of options of each to satisfy the various tastes but stay within your budget. Always supply plenty of juice, as well as soft drinks available for guests who aren't likely to consume alcohol.

Eggnog is an excellent choice to serve at Xmas celebrations and for an event with a mixer, you may need to hire a competent bartender to mix your drinks in your place. It is possible to select just two free alcohol beverages to serve and then stick with these. You can provide a wide array of garnishes available for guests to add to the mix drinks (such like olives, bits of fruit such as citrus such as celery sticks, strawberries or mint buds).

TIPS FOR HOLDING A KID'S CELEBRATION

A celebration with children could provide a great time or even a hassle, depending the way your plans are. Here are some suggestions to ensure that your child's party is enjoyable not just for your child but also for the host as well.

1. Keep the amount of people visiting at a minimum for children who are still young. The best practice is to allow for the amount of guests who are of the child's age.

2. Create a start time and end time as well as a surface times on the invitation. If you have children younger than that, two hours of celebration is sufficient.

Find out if your child are interested in an appropriate theme for their party. Make sure the space is decorated according to the theme and use the help of your child to get the event to go ahead.

If you want to add a flair for the event, give the food with intriguing names such as Shark Pearly whites sandwiches, Fairy Bread, Heart Hamburgers, Pirate Strike and so on.

It's not meant for people who are visiting, but to allow you to keep your the routine. 2:15 p.m. 2.15 pm, greet visitors and also socialize 2.15 pm, search for prizes; 2.45 pm, pin on donkeys; 3 pm, Magic Program; 3.40 pm, drink and eat the birthday pie at 4pm when visitors depart.

Instead of performing it is possible to hold a workshop with the kids. Incorporate this into the party's special occasions, specifically when it is in line with the theme.

Do you have any entertainment at home different from video games designed for children. It is possible to hire these entertainers or perform the house entertainment by yourself or seek assistance from your family or neighbours who might want to help with kids.

It is essential to ensure that you are able to have at least at least one other adult present who can help you during the event. Parents and their children may prefer to stay, particularly in the case of children.

9. There should be a variety of party drinks readily accessible to children when they go home. There is a possibility of incorporating of a sweet treat or something that fits the theme of your celebration.

10. Let your child write thank you notes (if older than) at the end of the celebration. This can help to remember how much fun he had, as well as the gifts that he received.

If you are hosting an event that are likely to offer alcohol, it is possible to make a variety of alcohol to suit the theme of your party or organize an Bring Your Own (Bring Your

Own) event. Eggnog is a great option to serve during Xmas celebrations and also when there is an alcohol event, you might have to engage professional barmen who are knowledgeable about mixing your drinks. If you are preparing drinks to serve at a children's party don't rely solely only on the soft drink. If you're having the event of a Tea Celebration for kids, provide their drinks with china mugs as well as food items. Make sure to decorate the space with the manner you want and ask your child's help to get their hands involved.

Chapter 4: The Best Ways To Arrange Your Celebration Preparations

The theme you choose will determine how you prepare. If you're planning to hold your event in outdoor location You will need to research how accessible the area is and also record the location. Make a spending plan overview including all expenses for the occasion, which includes invitations, decorations as well as food, drinks entertainment, rent prices and group hire (if you have any kind of).

When the RSVP date has passed you can count the number of guests who will be attending and also plan your menu for the celebration. If you're preparing food, think about what recipes you can make and then iced-up to make it easier.

Create a budget synopsis including all costs of the party, which include invites, invitations, design as well as food, drinks and entertainment costs, as well as rental fees as well as group hiring (if you have any). If you're preparing the food menu for your event, think about the dishes that can be prepared or iced prior to the event.

Be sure that you are able to ensure that the RVSP day is clearly important as it gives plenty of time to accommodate the volume of people who will be attending. If you buy more than the course of time, your budget could not seem as stretched.

If you plan your event early enough it will not only lessen stress, but you can also save money. If you're the kind person who has a tendency to throw many parties, this could be an ideal way to begin the preparations for your party as you are able to shop for the essentials to have a party during the entire year and find deals when they become available. When you know that you'll organize your first gathering, it is time to begin your preparation activities.

If you organize your party properly in advance it will not only lessen stress, but you can also save cash. If you're the kind person who has a tendency to throw many parties This is a fantastic method to begin planning your party as you are able to shop for the essentials needed to host an event during the entire year and also take advantage of bargains as you come across the opportunity.

Don't leave it until just a few weeks prior to your event or you may discover that you're looking for has recently been snapped up. Certain performers have a schedule that is at least a month in advance, therefore be ready to start this early, or you could miss the opportunity to be missed.

Call the rental business at least a few days in advance of the date to inquire about timings for distribution, and make sure that you receive the proper assistance required in establishing any equipment. Be sure your attire you choose is well-organized and allow enough time prior to the party to have your own ready to host the event. If you've prepared thoroughly, you'll enjoy the party for as long as you have guests!

THE BEST WAYS TO STRATEGY AN ELEVENTH HOUR MIXER

Three elements must have to put together an efficient cocktail party in the last minutes with guests, a fully-equipped bar and also an enjoyable feeling! There is a limited amount of time to plan the event with mixed drinks and also you will not have enough time to prepare and mail invitations. Events with alcohol typically last about two hours so you should give guests a start time as well as a finish.

If you're throwing your alcohol-related event in connection with the occasion (the Oscars, the Races, Election Day) after the event, your signature alcohol drink could be a fit to your theme. These drinks will come in handy next time you want to hold a mixed-drink occasion!

Three essential ingredients that you need to throw together an excellent last minute alcohol event: visitors as well as a bar that is equipped as well as a sense of fun! There is a limited amount of time left to organize the event of your choice but not sufficient time to plan and send out invitations.

Make sure to contact everyone who you would like to greet. Cocktail parties generally take 2 hours so you should give your guests with an opening and a finishing time.

2. Create a list of each detail that needs to be accomplished so you will be focused.

Do you have any kind of snacks in your refrigerator freezer? If not, you'll need certain snacks can be made easily or buy from a shop. When you've been able to contact your guests select your meal option (maintain the process simple) and then go to the store for the food you need.

Set up a bar in order to provide the drinks. Get a bartender on board or one of the guests prior to the event whether they'd like to be a barman. As it is a celebration that has to be last minute, it is possible to opt to ask a friend who is a great one.

Pick a few of drinks with alcohol to be served. If you're planning to throw an party with alcohol due to the occasion (the Oscars, the Races, Election Day) after it, perhaps your favorite alcohol drink could fit with your fashion. These drinks will come in handy the next time you make the decision to hold celebrations with mixed drinks!

6. If you are unable to establish an alternative bar, as well as you don't plan to serve anything extra elaborate than sparkling wine, there is a chance to use by using a colder with ice for drinks. It is a great option if you drink your mixer outdoors during summer.

Make sure your house is clean prior to the party. Drinking events for alcohol are about engaging with others, not to hide within an area of sharpness.

8. You can fill all the trays with ice and make sure you ice the day up when you have had time.

9. Pick the most appropriate songs for your mixer. You should also set it on before guests arrive.

10. Dress in your alcoholic beverage dress and get ready for the attend the event!

TIPS FOR HIRING PERSONNEL FOR YOUR EVENT

Some party-goers believe that the sole method to have fun and appreciate the event is by utilizing a staff to manage the celebration. Other artists would prefer doing it by themselves. If you're working in a group for a celebration, There are many things to consider:

What amount of your budget plan do require to employ staff? Once you have a clear idea of what you are able to spend then you can decide upon the requirements to host your celebration.

2. How many people do you need? The event personnel can be a lot of and diverse as well as comprise these:

a. Occasion Planners

b. Team members to be set up from the Event Equipment-hire shop

C. Barman

d. Food caterers

e. DJ/Band

F. Performers

g. Wait personnel

H. Butlers (for extremely official events).

i. Clean-up team.

Make sure you have your staff members on hand in advance of the date for your event. They may have great suggestions for your celebration. Would you like them to be dressed to match the fashion of the occasion or keep it simple with a the black and white look?

What are the best places to find a trustworthy party team members? Did you attend a great celebration, where everyone performed flawlessly? Examine the documents for your region and also search on the internet for teams in your area.

If you're planning to have the event catered, try the recipes before selecting a caterer for food. It is important to ensure that it is as delicious as it appears!

6. Talk about the types of music you want to hear with your DJ, particularly when your event is based on some theme. Don't want to dance to hip leaps at a 50s rock and roll party.

7. If you're using delay teams be sure you've enough for the number of people who will be attending the party. Another thing you'll need is a tense team trying at feeding excessive people within short time.

8. If you are working with musicians at celebrations for children, check their references. It is best to observe them perform before you hire the performers.

9. You should eliminate the hours employees will definitely have to work. Be sure to thank them after the day for work that was well-done.

10. Let loose and enjoy the fact having no need perform the work since you've actually paid someone who else will do the job!

Some party-goers' most effective way for them to relax down and enjoy their party is to collaborate together with staff members to make the most of the event. If you plan collaborate with a staff member at your celebration, here are some things to consider:

Are you a part of an amazing event at which your team performed perfectly? Make sure you satisfy your team before the event day. If you're using delay workers be sure you've got enough to meet the requirements of people attending the celebration.

TIPS FOR EMPLOYING A CATERING SERVICE FOR YOUR CELEBRATION

When you're hosting catered events at your own home or in a location for a party it is essential to make sure you are getting the best standard of service as well as the trustworthiness and credibility of the catering staff that you hire. Here are a few tips to keep in mind when looking for a catering company:

Examine the course and also the interaction of the catering staff. Does it suffice to meet your needs?

2. Make sure they've all of the required documents, including insurance policies health licenses, insurance policies and the appropriate licenses required for the job.

3. If you're hiring them to manage a place, make sure that they are familiar with the operational processes at the site.

Discuss exactly what the percentage of people who will be waiting for the waiter will be. Check out how your team is likely to dress, and should you have any type special requirements regarding their attire (such for a fashion party).

Does it have to be a sit-down affair in which guests are served a food or is it the type of event where guests are served buffet style? Catering for an event needs to be aware of this to cater the appropriate menu.

Inform your caterer about the budget you have set to get their suggestions. In addition to food, it can also comprise dishes and flatware rental as well as beverages, corkage cutting cakes, solution cost, table design Bartender, setting up and clear-up services. Some food caterers can't offer everything, but some do provide all of the above.

5. If the guests have special dietary needs, are they suitable for the event? Be sure to provide these details from the catering service well ahead of time.

6. Contact the catering services for the timetable to host the event. What types of courses will be available and for how many days between each program?

the caterer for your meals on your budget to find their suggestions. The food caterer should be able to supply an agenda of events to be held. The agreement should include any equipment leasings the caterer will offer including table layout as well as dishware, tables, chairs. The caterer and the host and host need to know the various aspects of having an efficient event.

The contract should also contain any rental of equipment that the caterer can include, for example dishes, tables table and chairs. It is essential to ensure that the cost of overtime for employees are covered in the event that your party will be scheduled for overtime along with the cancellation program.

Check that your catering company has everything in order. The catering company as well as the host need to know everything in order to ensure a smooth celebration.

Catering companies must be aware of this information to plan the proper way.

Chapter 5: Tips For Developing A Perfect Seats Prepare For Your Event

How many weddings were feared to be cancelled because the groom's mother won't rest after to the father of the bride's future husband? There's always the problem of a strange Auntie Helen who will sit next to her and also be astonished by her peculiar behavior or even a complete stranger smell? Try these suggestions to help make sure that the resting place is according what follows:

1. If you are planning a small dinner party, be sure that your host sits near the kitchen area to ensure easy access.

Consider all the people you have and any sort of peculiar behavior they may exhibit. Find out what they do to be more social in which way and get your visitors to sit down. Begin with the primary people at dinner like the guest of honor, or your supervisor and then place guests next to your host.

2. Other people to consider resting near the host include those who are new or have a quieter visit. In this way, the host can ensure that they're part of the conversation.

3. Try to rest and also keep people with just one person you know. It is not a good idea to allow anyone to become negative.

4. A few people like to be in separate couples to get together with their friends. It also helps with music to ensure that they don't appear like a lone person in the crowd.

5. If your guests are all up, consider the possibility of letting them relax wherever they would like to. If you're hosting a number of irritants, you can use the location card to ensure that they sit where you want they should be.

6. If your dinner event is larger in comparison to just one table, you should consider having guests move chairs between shows. In this way, guests are

bound to mix because no one will be able to occupy an entire table.

7. If children are included sleeping on their own table, along together with other young guests. It will give their moms and dads with a break, and they will have plenty of fun playing with each with each other than settling in the company of boring adults!

8. In larger celebrations for instance wedding celebrations where guests are seated next to each the other around tables, as well as work colleagues on a second. If you see a lot of irregularities take into consideration that some of your guests are social and so, place them on tables with people who they may not have a good relationship with.

9. It's smart to include a mix of males and ladies sitting at tables in the ideal way. If you have guests who are older and have vision or hearing impairments, ensure the

table in a place where they can listen to speeches.

This is just a handful ideas to get you to where you want to be. You must be prepared for a variety of situations and remember that at larger events, there is a chance that you will not please all of the guests.

Another option to consider staying close to your host include beginners and quieter visitors. It is a good idea to try and rest your guests with at most one who they are familiar with. If your guests all get together, think about giving them the space to rest as they want. If the dinner event you are hosting has a larger size in comparison to a single table, think about moving seats between classes. If children are part of the group sitting at a different table than those who are older guests.

CONCEPTS FOR HOLDING AN OUTDOOR CELEBRATION

The spring and the summer time, when climate is favorable, outdoor occasions are great ideas. In addition to electrical storms no thing can ruin non-winded celebrations. Even in the event that rain is expected it is possible for the event to be moved within. Here are some tips to keep in mind while planning your outdoor event.

Outdoor events can have different styles. Think about the theme of your the event and also aim to enhance the theme.

2. In sending invitations, inform the guests if

Check beneath tables and chairs to check for crawlers as well for insects. People do not want to experience any kind of apprehensive shock crawling on their legs!

In order to keep the pesky flies out of food preparation, place a few pieces of bacon that are not far in the kitchen as well as from the place where food is consumed. It will surely draw the fly away from visitors.

For drinks that are delicious but accessible to guests make sure you fill a large container with ice. You can also place it on the table in the shade. What is the best way to use the wheelbarrow, an additional barrel, or even a reusing one?

a. It is sure to have a nighttime or daytime party, so people can get ready for sunshine or for a relaxing evening

b. They must dress in an image

C. They will provide the steaks they make and the drinks

Decorate with flowerpots, umbrellas as well as pillows to make it more a daytime event. Are you planning to use a theme of shade or towels, as well as the spheres of the coastline to decorate your pool party?

7. If you do not have adequate tables as well as chairs to accommodate your guests, You could spread carpets over the lawn in the form of a picnic. It will definitely contribute

to an untidy and unintentionally sloppy atmosphere.

Make sure your catering is simple for outdoor events. Dishes, treats as well as salsas are simple and simple to mix and match.

9. Play background music to your favourite theme. If your event is scheduled for the evening, guests might be inclined to dance, so make sure that the space is cleared for dancing floors.

10. Examine the projected during the day of the event. Also, prepare to move inside your house if the forecaster provides a negative prediction.

Springtime and summertime and when the weather can be favorable, outdoor parties are an excellent idea. Other than electrical storms no thing can ruin this loosening of the events. And should rain show in the future, the celebration could always be relocated to inside. Below are some suggestions to think about when organizing your outdoor party.

Take advantage of the casual atmosphere outdoor fun. If you're not, you may find that it winds as a regular event within your schedule for celebrations.

Outside parties can have different styles. Keep your catering menu straightforward for events that take place outdoors.

EVENT RULES FOR VISITORS

If you're not sure whether you're able to attend yet, you can still talk with the hosts. Do not ever dress up for an event and not let the host to know you're going to be there.

Similar to be sure to not invite guests who are not welcome to the party. If you're single and you are now that you are seated, it is possible to call the host and inquire whether you can invite your new friend, but you shouldn't feel cheated if you are told that they will not.

Being considered an excellent visitor is easy. Just following a couple of fundamental guidelines will ensure you get more invitations.

1. Always ask the host to bring any items for the occasion or help in any way. If you're requested to bring something in, ensure the item you are able to bring!

Make sure you arrive on time for dinner parties, but you might have a bit of flexibility in informal gatherings. If you're running behind, contact your host, and inform them when you anticipate you'll arrive.

Make sure to say hello regularly to your host and you may want to give them a small gift (unless the invitation specifically states present-free). When you are done, make sure the host is able to say goodbye.

2. If the code for an outfit has been formulated, then you can follow it. If you have a theme and you're certain what you need to go about getting it, phone the host to inquire the amount that is expected.

On the day, have a social gathering! The purpose of celebrations is to have fun and so be sure to register!

Avoid showing up to the party hungry, and, afterward, teasing everything in sight. Try not to get drunk. People who drink are embarrassed or cause damage at many events.

3. If your children have been received, ensure that they behave appropriately and also are fully aware of what the guidelines for your event are.

4. Don't ever be a slave to your hosts storage cabinets or rooms.

5. Offer to help your host with to clean.

7. Be sure to leave at the specified timing on the surface (or before if it is necessary). Don't overstay your welcome.

8. Contact them or write a thank you note within a week following the event.

9. Enjoy the celebration!

Don't ever go to an event and not let your host to know you're attending.

Similar to don't bring unwelcome people to an event. Always ask your organizer if you can contribute something to the celebration or assist with any way. Make sure you arrive on time for dinner parties, but you might find yourself a little flexible to more relaxed gatherings. The purpose of events is to have fun and having fun, so be sure to register!

CELEBRATION FAVORS YOUR VISITORS WILL CERTAINLY KEEP IN MIND

Provide your guests with personalized container labels or wrappers for sweets that include details of your evening's events. The tag can be comprised of the image of your guest or guest of honor.

A small gift from the event is sure to make the evening memorable especially if your event service is special. The best party favors don't have to be expensive, because there are many different options available when you conduct a little of research.

Just about any small present, it is possible to customize You just need to locate a service. If you think that you would like something customised however you aren't able to find an agent, try making these on your own or contact a professional willing to create the item specifically for you.

3. Provide each person with a chilled glass to enjoy the evening particularly if it matches the theme of the event.

If you're planning a sporting event, make sure you provide the guests you want to invite with the colors of your group or with logo designs. To promote specific sports activities, it is possible to try these: Golf imprinted golf courses with guest of honor's information. Auto racing, perhaps as a game automobile in the host's preferred color; Olympic Gamings; Gold medals engraved with the event's information.

5. Personalized napkins made of paper or owner of the location are always an adorable memento of the celebration.

6. Votive candlelights make fantastic tables and can also be used as a favor for the celebration guests. Candles with votive bulbs can be found in a variety of styles to fit the theme of your event.

7. If you're planning an Coastline event, a swimming pool or Caribbean occasion, be sure to welcome your guests by presenting them with a necklace of flowers or covers.

Chocolates that are delicious and sweet will always be a welcome support! Do you want them to be separate created?

9. An Xmas assistance could make a nice addition to the visitor's tree, or even making some home-made Gingerbread people.

10. Ton of cash cookies always a nice treat for your guests to receive. This could be an ideal part of the event in which everyone is able to review their money!

11. The perfect home decor accessories comprise of boxes filled with seeds individual sauces, mix packets, as well as tiny floral holders.

Votive candles create stunning design for tables as well as make great party favors for guests.

The list of party ideas is endless. Just be creative, and you'll come up with something that your attendees will definitely keep on their minds.

Giving your guests a small gesture from your event is sure to make the evening even more memorable; especially in the event that your party's services are in some way distinctive. Events do not have to cost a lot and there are a lot of different alternatives available when you do some study. If you're hosting an event based on sports, provide the guests you invite that feature your group's colors or designs of your logo in these. In case you want to promote specific sports activities, try the following options: Golf - imprinted golf spheres that include the guest of honor's details; Auto racing, possibly as a plaything vehicle with the host's preferred shade and Olympic Games and gold medals with the date of celebration.

Chapter 6: Importance Behind The Planning

From the beginning it is likely that you're asking your self why you need to organize a party. I have asked myself the same time and again over many years. The reason I was sure of it was because I always wanted similar great and enjoyable parties hosted by my mother.

I remember the events Mom held as a child. The thing I couldn't recall until later in life was the work that was put to almost every event she was hosting. People who attended her events were so fun. My older brother and I would get out of our rooms then walk to the top of the stairs, and then watch the crowd through the railing. We did this until we were arrested, often by my Dad. I always knew I wanted to get older and have amusement at my own birthday parties just like my Mother as well as my Father had when they were at their own.

It's one of the main reasons you should plan your event. Fun and thrilling parties will be discussed for months, and years. Another reason to organize your event is to ensure accidents. This can be devastating and embarrassing for you and unpleasant for guests if you don't have enough food and drink for everybody. Inadvertently inviting someone to your party may result in unhappiness or even loss of relationship. Insufficient funds to purchase everything you require can dampen the celebration. There are a lot of others that could happen to you. Make sure that you don't allow this to occur. You must ensure that everything runs well, so that your guests are having an unforgettable time. All you need is correct preparation.

While planning a party may be stressful and time-consuming, or even anxious, it's not required to trigger panic attacks. This is why the book was created. This book will help you with organizing every element of an event that is successful. Keep a calm mind, keep your sanity maintained, and act as an entertainer and hostess that enjoys hosting having their own celebration. Let's start with basic guidelines.

Chapter 7: Learning The Basics

If you are planning your own party, it is important to start at the start. Beginning with the basics of a good party plan.

#1 WHO - Who's this party for? Do you want to invite your boss or friend? Are you hosting it for a loved one or acquaintance?

#2 Why - Why are organizing a party? Most of the time you will find an occasion to throw the event. Are you throwing a party to commemorate an anniversary, birthday, the opening of an enterprise, or even the announcement of engagement, a an upcoming baby or you simply need to have a celebration. Later in the book, I'll explain the different reasons why you should have parties without any motive in the first place. Do you find this intriguing?

#3 What date and time are you planning to hold the celebration? Did you decide to set a time?

4. What is the location where the event is going to take place? If you've chosen the location, this will decide how many guests you are able to invite guests. Make sure to choose your venue carefully.

#5 What kind of event are you planning to have? It could be a formal dinner event (sit-down formal dinner or casual buffet) or a cocktail party wine tasting and cheese or meeting and meet and greet? The list is endless. Is there dancing going on at your event?

It is essential that you start by answering to the five basic questions since they'll help connect everything in the course of process of planning. The answers will aid in the foundation for the party's plan. In order to help guide you through the entire process I'm going to organize a party in steps. In this way, you'll be able to observe the flow of everything. This is where the real planning and having fun begin.

Side Note

My son Charlie will be turning 50 in the coming year. I've decided to make the birthday celebration he had to help you to organize your own event. It is possible that you are not planning the birthday celebration, but that isn't a problem.

Whatever type of gathering you're having, the fundamentals of your strategy are exactly the same. Therefore, I'll begin by answering five simple questions:

1. WHO will the event be for? It is a birthday party for my child Charlie.

#2 Why do you want to have this party? Charlie turns 50 in August.

#3 When will you be having the celebration? The party will be held for Charlie's birthday on August 5, 2019.

#4 Where will you be hosting the event? I've decided to choose for the American Legion

Post 372 in Cherry Hill, NJ as the location for this event.

#5 What kind of celebration are you throwing? I'm throwing Charlie the "Poker Party".

I've answered five questions that are the foundation of my study. It is now time to tie these answers in order to plan the real thing.

Chapter 8: Choosing The Perfect Theme

It's all good. Once I've got some basic ideas and ideas, I'm able to tie it all up in creating one amazing celebration. The theme for this party is to be one of a Poker Party to surprise my son for his birthday, which falls on the 5th of August.

The place you are located can make a difference on the amount of guests that you invite, which opportunities you have to take part in, and so on. I performed an local Internet search followed by a few calls, and then chose The American Legion Post 372 located in Cherry Hill, NJ. The Post is located close to our home and also to the friends of Charlie whom we will invite to the event. The hall is sufficient to hold the poker tables of 5-6 needed for the 50-60 players who attend the.

Selecting a theme could be essential to have a memorable celebration, but most often. Sometimes, however, themes are not required. These times will be discussed in the future.

I picked for a Poker Party because Charlie has been a fan of poker since the age of eight years old. As we stayed with my parents every weekend night on Fridays and Saturdays would have been "Poker & Daiquiri Night". Of of course, Charlie would only be served virgin cocktails as we did not play with actual cash. The first time we played, we used toothpicks and eventually moved to chips from poker. When we finished the evening, Charlie would get to trade in his chips to buy brand new books or toys of his preference. It was an enjoyable time to everyone.

If you're having difficulty picking a theme your celebration, do as I did. You should think about the reasons you're hosting a celebration or what you are hosting it meant for. The theme should be based on your food choices to serve as well as the interests or ages of the guests of honor.

Perhaps you have a particular film you like to watch or the food you enjoy to consume. Get your the family and friends to get together to enjoy "Trivia Night" or a "Pizza Party". There are many themes for your party. Get suggestions from family members and friends. suggestions or search for themes through the Internet. It's possible to be surprised by the ideas you come across. Then, in the book, I'll provide 110 party themes ideas. More than the amount of ideas you'll likely use over the course of a life time.

Chapter 9: Begin Preparations

I've got the fundamentals down. The next step is to apply those principles to planning the party. In the past it will be an easy step-by-step procedure guide to help you to follow. I will detail each step you need to follow, but not all the details like guest names, addresses, etc. Write down a list of the things you're planning. Use either a spiral notebook or the app you have on your computer. It is important to mark each item you check off as you go through the task. Also, it is recommended to prioritize your checklist. Begin with the things that must be accomplished 4-6 weeks prior to the date of the celebration, three weeks prior to the main celebration, two weeks prior to the event one week prior before the date prior to the event. At this point, everything will be completed and you're free to enjoy the party. There are a few of activities to take part in on the day of the event and the week following the celebration.

About 4-6 weeks before my birthday party, I will need to prepare the guest lists. I'm making the list of 50 to 75 guests to invite. Be sure to consider the dimensions of the venue in which the event will be scheduled to be held. Because everyone who you invite may not be in attendance, make sure to send your RSVP by providing your telephone numbers or email addresses to receive a reply. If you want to add a letter of back-up, but this will cost you extra because of postage and stationery. Vista Print is a great website for creating your own invitations, if you have time and money. But, you can also find an excellent invitation at Walmart or your local dollar shop.

This is a crucial element in planning a party. In this phase of planning, establish financial limits to you. If a person is assisting you with your finances, then be sure that you're in the same boat with regards to budgeting. Stay as true to your limits as you are able to. Do not run out of cash until you've got everything you require. Include the rental hall (deposits are reimbursed) cleaning up after your party (if the service is employed) as well as cleaning materials (if required) and food, caterer or and decorations, as well as rental equipment like chairs and tables (if they are not supplied by the venue) as well as any additional equipment needed to conduct planned events (I require poker chips and playing cards) Also obviously, entertainment (if you're using an entertainment company or DJ). Be sure to reserve entertainment 4 to 6 weeks prior to the event, as the schedules of entertainment companies are often booked rapidly. It is important to study agreements thoroughly, and request paid in cash receipts.

Within this time frame of 4-6 weeks it is important to determine what meals you'll serve your guests. Is it a formal meal or snacks? Are you drinking? What about drinks? American Legion is providing a waitress to provide drinks. The cost of the hall is inclusive of additional bartenders, an attendant, as well as the bar is portable and installed inside the hall. The guests can enjoy a three-drink minimum for our bill with any extra drinks being charged at the guest's expense. There is a person who owns an SUV and will take guests to the event and the same way. There are some guests who take rides together with an assigned driver.

I'm placing an purchase for the birthday cake, and purchasing all the party items approximately 4 weeks in advance. There is no car in my home which is why I prefer Amazon or Walmart to purchase my party items. There is a person I know who owned her own bakery. She provided the cake. If I tell her my requirements today, I give her enough time to have it prepared.

Chapter 10: Midway Through The Prep

It is clear that I have covered lots of topics. I'm not trying to overwhelm and confuse the reader with irrelevant information that you might not want to know for your gathering. However, I will be clear. In the final chapter of this publication, I'll provide a concise list that of guidelines to help you plan every type of party with any topic. As I said previously it will also include an entire list of 110 themes for your party. However, for the moment I'll continue to write with the same mindset as if I was making plans for my son's surprise 50th birthday celebration.

In this section I'll go over the things you need to do at the midpoint of planning around 2-3 weeks prior to when you are planning the "big day". About 3 weeks prior to the event, make the guest list, and then send invitations. Maintain a list of those invited on your telephone or computer, so that it is easy to cross each one off when they RSVP. It is important to provide a precise date and date when they need to respond with their RSVP.

This is an ideal opportunity to discuss the plans for the coming week. You should ensure you have all the supplies that you require. Invite family and friends to help out at the event for cleanup (unless you employ an experienced service) or other events (I require dealers to play at the tables for poker) as well as taking photographs (unless you employ an experienced photographer) as well as greeting guests in the entrance.

Two weeks before the date Call those who didn't RSVP to confirm that they are going to be there. Meet with staff to confirm that they'll be there. Delegate their duties to them. If you're having competitions, purchase and package the prizes to the winners. Make sure you confirm your cake's order as well as the entertainment. If you are hosting an adult event, you should find and employ a babysitter should you require it. It is important for you to be calm. Sure, your party is two weeks away and you're following the pre-planned schedule. This helps to run the event smooth and help keep the tension levels low. It's all under your control. YOU CAN DO IT!

Chapter 11: Review & Revise Plan (If Necessary)

It's almost the time to go. Only one day left until the big event. The party is slowly progressing and are running well. All is in order thanks to the preparation. The time has come to reflect on the progress made so to date.

Make use of the checklist gave at the end of the book to help you exam. Make yourself a cup tea or your favorite drink along with the checklist and the pen. Relax in a tranquil area, away from distracting or disruptive events. Take a moment to review what you've done in the last year. This is a listing of the things that should have been accomplished up until the present.

1. Selected a topic.

2. A guest list was created.

3. Select date and time.

4. Select and lock the place.

5. I ordered the supplies for the party.

6. Choosen the games or activities to play. games.

7. The activity was ordered and the game equipment.

8. The band was booked, the DJ, etc.

9. The invitations were sent out.

10. Family and friends were gathered to help with the celebration.

11. Contacted guests who didn't RSVP.

12. The cake was ordered (if you needed it).

13. We have confirmed the show.

14. Wrapped and purchased prizes (if relevant).

15. The sitter and I touched base.

Once you have reviewed your plan it is possible that it is necessary to revise your list. Things could have changed when you first started making plans. The sitter might have resigned, and you have to find an alternative. You might have accidentally crossed one off the guest list. Do not fret. There is still enough time to find another person. Contact the lost person and send a personalized invitation to the person. It's a full week away. There is still time to make any changes you've found in your analysis that you didn't think was finished or that needs to be addressed.

Chapter 12: Finalize The Plan

It is time to review your checklist and re-written the list (if required). This week, prior to the day of the celebration There are some more tasks which must be completed.

1. Confirm guests by calling them to inform them about the date and time. You should ensure that they are given instructions. Make sure that you remind those in need of transport if you provide transportation.

2. Buy camera batteries and film If needed.

3. Take a look at any items you might not have bought.

4. Buy the food items in advance, unless your party catering.

5. If you can, make your own games or crafts, and be sure to have everything required.

If you've adhered to the guidelines, you're ahead in the race and you will need to complete a few things in the final weeks before the celebration. Another reason to plan for a party is to plan things gradually. It will be easier to manage everything in the final second. After the week has ended, all will be ready to take place.

It's the day prior to the celebration and you'll be doing nothing.

1. Make any meal that could be prepared and then reheated. I chose to offer snacks to poker players. The players can eat chips, peanuts and candy and dips while playing poker. You can prepare whatever you've chosen to serve, if it is able to be made a day before.

2. Make the hall look nice and ask them to let you stay the night prior to. Then your assistants will come in handy.

Children love getting involved these kinds of activities. Therefore, if they're older enough to be able to assist bring them along. This is it. Our final prep is complete. Go to your home, have a nice bath and then get the rest you need in preparation for tomorrow's "big day".

Chapter 13: Party Time!

WOW! Take a look at the things you've accomplished over the past 4-6 months. Today is a big day. There's only a handful of tasks you'll need to complete this morning.

If you are hosting a birthday celebration, you should take the cake home or a cake that is taken away. If you're using balloons, make sure to blow them up before you put them up a few hours before the event begins. The best time to gather with your helpers approximately 4 hours prior to the party in order for the decoration along with food, snacks and prizes. put up. Be sure to prepare an area for presents that are brought to guests of honor to an event for birthdays.

The theme for the event will dictate what needs to be completed for the "big day". However, every party will be pretty alike in so far being set-up with food, decorations as well as the decorations. Make your own judgment on what you need to do within the planning timeframe of six weeks in accordance with what kind of celebration you're having. You're clever. Utilize the checklist as well as your basic sense. Contact me in the final section in the text. If you're unsure of anything, get in touch with me. I'll be glad to offer advice or recommendations. This book was purchased by you. In appreciation I'll be available for you 24 hours a day to help make your event a hit.

Congratulations! The party is officially underway. All the guests are here. It's time to join the celebrations and have fun. Don't forget, you're also hosting or hostess. It is important to ensure that you circulate throughout the celebration. Your guests will help keep food and beverages in good order and keep the party going. The DJ or band who you booked can keep the party going and your dance floor hopping. Take part in games and other activities. Have fun and have fun dancing. If guests are able to are able to see how much you're enjoying yourself and having fun, they'll have enjoyable too. It's your turn to dance the night away and let loose. It's PARTY TIME!

Chapter 14: The Party's Over

Congratulations! You just had an event that was successful. It was unique and enjoyable. The guests will talk about your party throughout weeks, days and possibly even for months. Do yourself a big hug. Doesn't that feel good? The preparations are over and the celebration was an absolute achievement!

There are few more things to complete. Most importantly do this: send thank you notes to those who brought gifts (if relevant). Send thank-you notes to all your volunteers. It is recommended to write notes in handwriting using nice stationery for an extra personal design. Then, you should take your plan checklist, notes that you took, receipts, and so on. Save them. Use an organiser for your pocket. It is also possible to put them in sheets protectors, and then put them in a three-ring binder. It is something that you might be able to reference in the event of a celebration. It is also possible to share this details with relatives or acquaintances who may seek advice from you about how to plan your own memorable party. Are you prepared to be an event planner? This is a future book.

Chapter 15: For No Reason At All

9 out of 10 times the event is planned and held for a certain purpose. But, this isn't often the case. There is no need to be able to justify the reason you organize a celebration. It doesn't need to coincide with the time of a celebration. You might just wish to have a get-together with your buddies or relax after a difficult week. Perhaps you're just feeling that you need to have a celebration. No big deal. Here are some ways to have a celebration without any reason whatsoever. Oh, and it doesn't require the same amount of preparation. Therefore, send an email or text your loved ones, pour the cork in the champagne, serve the cheese, crack open the bottle and enjoy the most memorable party ever for the simple reason that you have.

Here are some reasons to host a celebration for any reason:

1. The moon is full.

2. The Walking Dead is back with a brand new season in the show "The Walking Dead".

3. It's TGIF.

4. The divorce decree is complete.

5. Just cleaned up your home.

6. Finally, you cleaned your attic.

7. You have quit your job that you don't like.

8. The neighbor who is always a nuisance is leaving.

9. An old acquaintance is in town.

10. Your father wants you to meet his brand new girlfriend.

11. Just made the cake.

12. The first snow or rain of the year.

It's easy to know what you want to do. It is possible to plan a party in celebration of a certain event or with no purpose in the least. By preparing a few things for your spontaneous party, or a detailed plan to host a memorable party it is possible to throw the most memorable party ever. Start planning now and then relax!

Chapter 16: Theme Ideas

The fun starts now. You must decide on a theme to your event. Like we said, here are 110 suggestions for theme ideas for your party. They are a great way to get a head to get started. Make your own list of things to make additions to the list. They will get your thinking process going.

1. Margarita Party

2. 50's Sock Hop

3. Taco Party

4. Rumble in the Jungle

5. Harry Potter Magic

6. Luau Feast

7. Old Hollywood Glamour

8. A Little Bit of Blarney

9. 1001 Arabian Nights

10. It's the '90s

11. Back to the '80s

12. Backyard Carnival

13. Couples Only Dinner Party

14. Mexican Fiesta

15. Be a Princess for a Day

16. New England Clambake

17. Flower Power

18. Teen Slumber Party

19. Tailgate Party

20. Murder Mystery

21. White Elephant Christmas Exchange

22. Make Your Own Pizza

23. Come as You Were

24. Masquerade Ball

25. Cinco de Mayo Celebration

26. Wine & Cheese Tasting

27. Pancake Breakfast

28. Potluck Dinner

29. Oscars Night

30. 007 Party

31. Cupcake Wars

32. Gangster Party

33. Roaring 20's Dance

34. Bollywood Bash

35. Toga Party

36. Family Game Night

37. Blind Wine Tasting

38. Mardi Gras

39. Karaoke Contest

40. Trivia Night

41. Havana Nights Cuban Fiesta

42. Decorate the Christmas Tree

43. Scotch & Chocolates

44. Seeing Red

45. Winter Wonderland

46. Beer Bash

47. Roaring 20's Speakeasy

48. Backyard Picnic

49. Formal Tea Party

50. Start A Book Club

51. Out of This World

52. Let Freedom Ring

53. Ugly Christmas Sweater Party

54. Disney Through the Ages

55. Pajama Party

56. March Madness

57. Rock Star Night

58. School Spirit

59. Family Movie Night

60. DIY Spa Day

61. Pretty in Pink

62. Texas Hold 'em Poker Night

63. Monster Mash

64. Bingo Bash

65. Formal Italian Dinner

66. 'Come as You Are' Birthday

67. Welcome Home

68. Black & White Ball

69. Pool Party

70. Country Western Dance

71. Casino Night

72. Go for the Gold

73. Alice in Wonderland

74. Pirate Bash

75. Disco All Night Long

76. Campfire & Smores

77. Easter Egg Hunt

78. Fall Harvest Dinner

79. Lord of the Rings

80. Truth or Dare?

81. Wizard of Oz Fantasy

82. Fashion Show

83. English Pub Luncheon

84. Sadie Hawkins Dance

85. Oktoberfest

86. Superhero Party

87. Christmas in July

88. Cabaret Night

89. I Love New York!

90. Bon Voyage

91. Wild, Wild West

92. Vampire Ball

93. Crazy Outfit Party

94. Mad Men Cocktail Party

95. Lawn Party

96. Cruise Ship Theme Party

97. Woodstock '69

98. Steampunk Party

99. Charity Chinese Auction

100. Family Fun Night

101. Scavenger Hunt

102. Milestone Birthday Celebration

103. Star Wars Theme

104. Minecraft Birthday Fun

105. Chili Cook-Off

106. Enchanted Forest Adventure

107. Recipe Exchange

108. Naughty or Nice?

109. White Party

110. Long Distance Baby Shower

Chapter 17: Choosing The Type Of Party

Each hostess or host enjoys seeing their guests have fun at their event. And so did I. I felt proud in making certain that every guest at my was having a great time. In the end, that's the point of an event - to enjoy fun together with others entertaining and to be amused. After a time I started to be less and less able to throw a party at the house. I was beginning to doubt myself. Why would I put forth all the effort, pay my money and invest my time to make everyone satisfied? No one of my acquaintances goes the extra mile to throw great events. What is the reason I should?

After a couple of months I realized that I wasn't selfish. I was just tired. I had enough of going out to the store to buy things for the party, and of cooking all day before the event, and of tidying off the mess. This is the moment I asked me if I could throw an event if you did not need to shop or cook? The answer was yes! I'd love to! This was the first step of figuring out how to throw an incredible celebration without spending an arm and a leg and consuming myself to the limit. I swallowed my pride and asked my people to lend me a hand. When they assisted me, I ensured I was enjoying ourselves. I started using the items I already had in my home more frequently, which reduced my budget for parties by a significant amount. Also, it saved me some visits to the stores.

It is now clear that you can throw an amazing event on a budget, without wasting entire hours of planning. In this guide I show the ways you can reduce the amount of work, costs while still providing a memorable event to each guest attending any party you host.

xxx

In order to make the party enjoyable First, choose the type of event you would like to host. It is crucial as it will create the atmosphere for your party and plan plans in accordance with the theme. For a simple party you can use a template it will show you what you'll need to accomplish for a great event! This is my invitation template that I'll share for you below. Once you have a plan set up, you don't have to do anything to make yourself a top host!

One of the first questions you should think about is: What kind of gathering would I like to throw? Here are a few examples can be used.

1. Dinner Party

What person wouldn't want to go to dinner parties? The appeal of candles and the snoozy hours in the evening when you're at your most at ease. If you enjoy cooking like I do, then you'll equally enjoy making the food as sharing it at your table with guests. It is easy to imagine me preparing my delicious meals that I'll serve my guests. From the appetizers and desserts I certainly enjoy making my own meals. pick. In order to reduce the amount of chores and chat with your buddies in the kitchen as you make the preparations for the event invite a few people from your circle to join you to assist during the cooking. It could be a sort of party pre-party. By utilizing this method of this, you will not be tired, and you'll be more relaxed as the event gets underway.

If you are worried that preparing an entire meal would take too much burden, then you can invite that your guests bring only one food item. A superb wine selection and expertly prepared drinks will make your event a hit.

2. Karaoke Party

Everybody loves to sing. even if they'd rather not. When they drink a glass of the alcohol, they'll get a microphone and sing to the tune of their heart's desire. It is possible to rent an online karaoke machine and it's a little expensive, or borrow one from a close friend. Create pica-pica dishes like onion rings, nachos fries, calamari, mozzarella sticks, and pizza. All of these are great to pair with a beers to increase your confidence when hitting those top notes.

3. Game Night

Go to the most eagerly anticipated championship game together with your most cherished group of friends, and show your support for your favourite team. You can also invite guests to attend the PPV Boxing Match, and as a reward, they may decide to bring refreshments and food for the gathering to enhance the excitement! The feeling of cheering on your team with your buddies rather than watching alone is more entertaining. Also, it's an ideal idea to use a borrowed projector to place the projector on a wall to create an even bigger screen.

4. Themed Birthday Party

Hosting a birthday celebration from the convenience of your own house will help you save lots of money renting a location for the party. Additionally you could also pick your theme for the party. This makes your event more personal. If you are hosting a party for kids, invite your child to watch their preferred cartoon series and have the guests (just the children for this party) to dress up in various characters from the show. If you're planning to host the event for a large number of guests, it is possible to choose two or three cartoons.

Adults can pick the most popular color film, music and so on. You can also select the typical themes such as the 1980s, western or nautical.

Template

Use this template only as a guideline for your event. Make note of the details you prepared your party. If, for example, you were playing Frank Sinatra and Dean Martin during a dinner event, the information it is recorded under Entertainment under the heading of Dinner Party so that the next time you have the opportunity, you could or repeat the show with a different group of guests, or alter the music. Be sure to record details in the log at every gathering you have. It is then possible to combine and mix, take away the items, then add more, and repeat. It allows for planning to be very simple.

Chapter 18: Picking Up Eatables

Organising a party can be difficult and tiring. The first step is be aware of the kind of celebration you're planning to have. You must then move your furniture around to provide maximum room and ease Also, consider a second glance at your decorations. Most importantly it is important to prepare tasty food that makes your event unforgettable.

When you are preparing food to serve at a gathering when planning a party, it is essential to take into consideration the age range of the guests.

1. If children will be in attendance:

Food servings must be in smaller portions.

Fruit juice, milk and chocolate beverages must be consumed, and

The sweets buffet can bring a smile to the faces of children.

2. If an elderly person is at the scene:

It is essential to eat vegetarian dishes.

Olive oil is recommended to cook

Fruits are a major success, particularly for those who have a restrictive eating plan or have a health-conscious mindset.

To help you get an idea of what foods you could serve your guests, here are a few recipes that are easy to prepare and I strongly suggest. The list starts with the appetizer, and will end with dessert.

Appetizers

1. Speedy Smoked-Salmon Crackers

I love the way that the cheese goes well with the salmon. Everybody would enjoy this.

2. Goat cheese-stuffed mushrooms

It's impossible to go wrong with a meal filled with cheese.

3. Southwest Egg Rolls

The flavor is hot. It's a great meal to get you started on your journey to a better appetite.

Soup

1. Wonton Soup

Just the right amount of salt This soup will get your stomach ready for the main meal.

2. Simple Chicken Noodle Soup

Each ingredient in this bowl complements one another.

3. Creamy Onion Soup

The perfect soup for the cold winter months the soup is somewhat thicker consistency.

The main dish could choose to serve 3-4 dishes made of beef, pork, seafood and fish. There is also pasta dishes that is essential for any gathering because people are awestruck by the taste!

Pork

1. Pork Tenderloin and Honeyed Butter

I love the sweet and buttery sauce, which adds flavour to tenderloins.

2. Pork Chops and Herb Stuffing

Foods that are filled with stuffing always manage to entice me when compared with the standard meals because you are curious about what it might taste like.

3. Zesty Pork Ribs

It could be among the meals that will be the talk of your guests.

Fish

1. Bacon wrapped cod and Frisee

It's a sinful, tasty recipe. The addition of bacon to a dish will always result in deliciousness.

2. Panko-crusted, fried fish sticks served with the herb sauce for dipping.

Another favorite among everyone of all age groups. It should be properly cooked so that you get that crisp exterior and deliciously moist and succulent fish in the middle.

Chicken

1. Grilled chicken Paillard served with a mint salad

Paillard means pounded meat. Since the meat is pounded it is a delicious delicacy that is soft. Without or with the salad, it's ideal for those who are health conscious.

2. Smoky Chicken Tacos

The kids and their parents will definitely return for more.

Beef

1. Seared Sirloin Steak With Onion Relish

Best cooked medium rare. This juicy and tender cut of meat is bursting with flavor and you'll want to know how to cook it.

2. Country Beef Brisket

I am a huge fan of beef. It's that tenderness and deliciousness which makes you want to eat to eat more and more.

Pasta

1. Macaroni and Cheese

The classic song will make an impact at any party.

2. Chicken Fettuccini along with Pesto Cream Sauce

Another recipe for healthy food that blends the taste of a healthy dish with. The creamy sauce is what your kids are sure to love it.

A Sweet Ending

In the end, this is the thing people are looking forward to.

1. Spring Shower Almond Petit Fours

It is tempting to snap a picture prior to enjoying the delicate flavor.

2. Mini Eclairs filled with Strawberries and cream

This is the bite-sized version of the crowd-pleasing.

3. Phyllo Cups are topped with Cappucino Cream

It's a macho dessert. Everyone is welcome to sample this delicious dessert.

If you're not interested in cooking, you could prefer to buy pre-made meals at the supermarket or could also request a takeaway from your favourite restaurant and cook it at your home. It'll reduce the amount of work you have to do and ensure that your guests are happy and eager to come back for more.

Chapter 19: Rearranging Furniture

Are you planning an event for your birthday friend or family member, or perhaps a reunion with your college pals or a basic celebration for your child's graduation from University? It is possible to change from a great event to a memorable one by changing your furniture?

The best way to make this simple gathering simply changing the arrangement of your furniture by adding lighting that will fit the mood for your gathering and setting decor that you can find in your home. In order to help you create an elegant and comfortable setting that maximizes the usage of your space these are some suggestions:

Make Interaction Easy

Set up your furniture in the way that your guests are able to talk and get involved with one another

For almost all occasions there are people who form small groups of around four or five persons. It can cause a lot of discomfort because seating arrangements don't permit an entire group to be able to effectively communicate between each other. In order to provide guests with seating arrangements that permit the group to have prolonged conversations and be comfortable, you should arrange your furniture in a way at least four out of five persons can sit an appropriate distance from one others and be able to see everyone within the group. It is possible to achieve this by creating a half-moon or full moon (of course, having enough room to move around the area) by arranging your seating arrangements.

Half-moons are preferred for those who change their groups. If your group of friends have a common interest, the half moon is more appropriate since they'll want to be able to connect with larger numbers of people in your party. If on contrary there are six to seven people who have known the other and have no one other than them, it's time to enjoy an entire moon. Utilizing throw pillows for an extra seating space creates a feeling of relaxation and creates a fresh place to sit in the area. There are a variety of carpets and set up at least four cushions in order for making an inviting seating space.

Placement of Decoration

Lighting fixtures that are appropriate to the theme or mood of the event.

To host a lavish dinner party put candles on the dining table to give the look of a sophisticated dining enjoyment. The carved and stained candles will help make the table appear (and the smell!) grand.

Making use of artificial or real flowers to your centerpieces is an excellent idea. There are even synthetic or dead scented flowers to decorate the home. Move it over on the table to put them on the table in a pleasing manner, and then you're done! Arranging a basket full of fruit is another good option.

If you are planning an evening party after dinner with drinks and cocktails served, lower the lights and string small rattan ball strings that have colored lights in the walls to create a tone for the evening.

Positioning the Buffet Table

Be sure to avoid placing the buffet/cocktail table against the wall.

I believe that putting the buffet table on the wall will limit the area that guests are able to serve themselves. Essentially, it cuts access to one end that of the table. If you're hosting an intimate gathering for up or 10 guests, it is possible to place the table in front of the wall. However, when you host larger gatherings, it will only limit your access to table. A minimum of one meter between the table and table allows for easy accessibility without taking up too much room.

As well as seating arrangement, you'll have to create a buffet or cocktail table attractive. It is obvious how important food is in any party. It is possible to ask your friends for help in selecting the tablecloth, vases for flowers and candle holders, for example. You could even borrow things from your acquaintances if they don't already have it or it would be too costly. Simple tablecloths will add a stylish appearance to the buffet table when you choose the appropriate colors and the right lighting.

Food that you cook looks better when it is served on an elegantly decorated table. There is plenty of room for everything the food items you need to place on your table and add aesthetics by placing objects. When placing utensils on the table put them in an order that they appear well-organized and take up a suitable quantity of space.

There are several ways to make the party a success for all. You've realized that to host an amazing party. You are not required to pay any money. The only thing you'll need is think of brilliant ideas for how you can utilize what you have and seek help when you need it.

Chapter 20: Make It Collaborative

As with any occasion it requires everyone's efforts for it to succeed. The process of planning a party on your own can be exhausting. If you decide to try everything on your own, you might be exhausted by the time the party starts! Be an absolute perfectionist but seek assistance from loved ones and your friends. Create a whole day of working in a team. If you can do this, you'll save energy and time, and while doing it you are able to get more ideas and concepts that your coworkers will develop. In addition, instead of being on your own in the process of preparing it's more enjoyable and enjoyable to be working as you chat with your friends.

Brainstorming

In order to gather ideas You can discuss ideas with your pals. The things you may brainstorm about are themes, menus decor entertainment, seating, as well as the time of the event. Invite your guests to take control of the decision making process. Allow them to be in control and grant them to be free. Keep notes down and listen to all remarks and suggestions. Then you will notice how swiftly the process is completed.

One of the things is most likely to require assistance for is food. Ask your guests for suggestions on recipes that you can include in the menu of your celebration. It is possible to ask your guests to bring drinks to the evening and then pay for catering, or you can host your own potluck, and then assign each dishes that everyone must bring to the event. They can also be asked to cook their favourite dish.

Steps of Planning

A little bit of making plans will allow you cut down on time preparing for your day. What you must accomplish is prioritize your items and write them down. Make sure to mark the tasks you finish immediately after they're completed so that you are able to proceed to the next crucial project.

You can create a list using the templates below. Prioritize the top task, and then from there. Each task must be assigned different ranking.

Template

This template allows it is possible to change the order of your tasks, without affecting your checklists. The benefit of having lists and rankings is that you are able to at only a glance know what you have to complete in the present. If, for instance, you've outlined 12 tasks that you've completed seven then you could simply be reviewing the ranking to take the eighth most crucial job you have to complete. Eliminating the items on a list creates the process confusing and chaotic. It is therefore recommended to prioritize and record while by using a method that the process clearer and more easy for your.

Gathering Materials

When all preparations are completed, you can begin collecting the items that are needed - food, fresh food, decorations and tissues. There is also the option of adding some exciting things that will bring the party to life for example, a karaoke machine. Request your guests to look for a cheap karaoke device on rent, or, better yet you can borrow one from a friend that has one.

Another alternative is to ask DJs to perform for your celebration. Also, inquire with your friends to let you know if they know of a DJ who might be able to play for the party at no cost in a brief amount of time in the event that it is not for the whole length of your party.

Delegate Responsibilities

The day before the celebration, you can ask your guests to assist you to cook the food. It is possible to have several people taking charge of various tasks so that they don't have to feel overwhelmed. It's crucial to ensure that both you and your guests are enjoying the process of preparing the event equally as the party itself. For a fun and enjoyable preparation Mix work and play. Sing songs, act out parts, gossip. If you are willing to help and assistance, you could also assist them with planning of the party.

Make Work Fun

By working with others, you could transform work into a fun experience. The best way to do this is instead of doing everything by you. It saves time, energy and cut costs in addition to having an enjoyable time with your buddies!. Additionally, having friends helping you with the arrangements also lets you build a bond and increase the bonds you share.

Chapter 21: How To Scent The Air For A Party

A few hours before the event Everyone is likely working on decorating the space and setting up furniture and cooking food. It is also the time when you are able to not think about the air quality in your home. The cooking process can produce smoke as well as the scent of cooked food, regardless of whether the exhaust fan is turned on. For getting rid of the smell, employ these methods:

Shut all the windows or doors to ensure that the odor would slowly disappear.

Use an air purifier

Prepare a potpourri for the stove top and place the leftovers, such as citrus, lemons bay leaves along with cinnamon sticks, cloves and other spices in a large saucepan of water. Let it simmer. Turn the heat down and stir often. The result will give you a refreshing smell that can mask your unpleasant smell in the kitchen.

Once the unpleasant smell is disappeared, put up scented decors to create an inviting scent to the house. You can do the following:

Scented Candles You can use them in the center of each table at the event. The candles can be lit up to create the mood of your event.

Aromatherapy Oil Burners are able to purchase various oil scents on the internet or in department stores. Aromatherapy oils are wonderful to smell and they can provide a great sense of relaxation.

Fragrance Incense Sticks - These have a pleasant scent when they are lit but they also create a bit of smoke.

Freshly picked flowers. vase full of gorgeous flowers won't just look gorgeous, but will also give off an exquisite scent.

Although you may have smelled your air prior to the commencement of your party It could be your air nature of the scent may change. There are guests who may have a habit of smoking. To get rid of the smell smoking cigarettes, particularly when you have kids pregnant women, or people that are susceptible to smoke at the event, put up a sign that prohibits smoking at the entrances to the smoking areas, or remind those who smoke to not use outside in the open or smoking zone. If you are not keen the guests to be disturbed by smoking regulations, you can install air fresheners inside the air conditioner.

A spray of fragrance is probably the most effective method to scent the air. In addition there are other options to make use of these items that will constantly scent your air

Essential oil Electric Diffuser. It constantly diffuses a scent, and covers the unpleasant scents. Simply plug it in, and then you're finished!

Potpourri is the best - nothing beats potpourri. It's an excellent decor and can also scent the air. The dried, naturally aromatic leaves are able to be placed in a glass or wooden bowls as centerpieces on tables.

If you're on a tight budget, you could create your own air fresheners.

Mason Jar Air freshener - Mix baking soda with essential oil in an empty mason Jar. Cover the lid with newspaper that has been punctured multiple times using a needle. This allows air to flow through. Put a ribbon around the neck of the jar to make it more attractive. (Note that baking soda can be an excellent natural deodorizer)

Fragrance Stones Place scent oil and colour into boiling water. Mix it until it is well mixed. Pour it into an empty bowl containing flour, salt and cornstarch. The mixture should be stirred until sufficiently thick to create the dough. The dough should be kneaded until it is smooth. Shape the dough into small chunks and allow it to dry.

Chapter 22: The Mistakes To Avoid

Hosting a gathering at the home is easy by planning a bit. The things require planning include:

The list of guests you'll be inviting based on the area you've got and

Making the menu will be the most crucial aspect of the celebration and also the most difficult to make a decision

Designing the decor as well as the setting, food, the music as well as the lighting.

Any time you attend a party it is possible to encounter difficulties and disputes. If you are aware of them and are prepared, you will be able to prevent them from happening to ensure that every event is smooth. It is easy to put too much pressure upon yourself if you think that you will be able to have the perfect celebration. Once you've done everything you are able to do, take a break. Check out some potential party spoilers. those mistakes that could ruin an excellent event.

1. Awkwardness

It's been a pleasure to invite some of your acquaintances, your schoolmates as well as from work neighbors. It is possible that the guests you invite don't meet each other. This could lead to awkwardness in the event that they're not introduced by the host or don't agree with one another.

It is important to introduce everyone to the other guests shortly after the guests arrive. This will allow everyone at your gathering be comfortable. If you find that there are some members of your group who are not able to get along with one another, you could either not have the group interact for too long or put them in separate areas.

2. Not enough food

In the course of planning, you have to know the amount of guests who will be attending your event. Also, you should consider the fact the fact that those you invite could bring a guest who is not invited. To ensure that you don't run empty-handed due to the fact that more guests attended the party than planned, ensure you've got dishes that will be sufficient even in the event that you were expecting guests or party goers to show up at your event.

3. Overspending

It is likely that you want to become known as the best host or an perfectionist. If you're organizing or planning the event you are planning, you could wish to make sure everything is flawless. The best DJ, stunning strobe lighting, an elegant karaoke machine that has all of the audio systems and on. It's normal, and even expected. Every time we perform things, we expect that it be of the highest quality. This is what we call quality and in addition to getting it correct, you must also be able to stay within the budget you have set.

There's one problem: it's important to not go over the budget you have set. Noting down every expense made on purchasing things for your event is an excellent way to help you remember the amount you will spend for the items you want to purchase. When you are in the middle of the planning and you realize that you're in risk of spending more than the budget you have set, think about borrowing the items from family and friends or consider alternative options that cost less.

4. The time of the celebration

The time for the event is usually preceded by "onwards" in an invitation. This informs the guests to be there for all they like. If you wish for guests to depart on the time (whatever date you consider appropriate) due to some reason, make sure you mention the date when the party is scheduled to end. This will be clear to guests at what time they can expect your party to come to an end. If you're not handing an invitation in paper or via electronic or even announcing the event to guests on the phone, then it is possible to suggest the conclusion of the celebration on the invitation.

Chapter 23: Preparing Cocktails

It's fun to host a party and entertaining, but nothing beats amazing cocktails to enjoy at the party. It is possible to lease a mobile bar equipped with unlimited beverages or create an own bar. Bars are ready. You could ask a person who is skilled at making stunning cocktails to help in the kitchen or to share recipe ideas. Be sure the bartender, no matter who they are, is aware of the tricks of his trade.

If you are able to find assistance or guidance, then you can read online for tips on how to create several popular cocktails. You should remain with the recipes you already know rather instead of experimenting. If a close acquaintance of yours is able mix drinks, it is possible to invite them over at the beginning of the evening and mix a couple of drinks. This allows you to understand what the cocktails will taste. It is possible to make changes and make sure that you have the perfect cocktail ready to serve at your next celebration.

If you are planning a party Try these cocktails (Keep your mind on the temperature!):

The best cocktails to enjoy during winter months and for the festive season.

Cane Cocktail - Candy Cane Cocktail - This is an amalgamation of candy cane crushed, strawberry vodka white creme de-menthe and cranberry juice, which gives you a slight sweetness.

Berry Little Cocktail - A cocktail of cranberries, sugar grapefruit vodka, Champagne, juice of cranberries, and Black currant juice. You can expect it to be tart and will be asking for more.

Eggnog Martini Drink that's frothy made up of cornstarch, sugar, ground nutmeg, pumpkin pie spice, milk in whole egg yolk, and brandy.

The Blizzard Cocktail - This drink is an extremely easy to mix cocktail composed consisting of Irish whiskey, or rum Hazelnut liqueur Irish cream hot coffee, liqueur and whip cream. It's very chocolaty!

Winter Solstice Cocktail - It could appear plain, however it is made with a variety of different ingredients, including the orange-flavored liqueur, orange vodka along with lemon and club soda. Add mint leaves and an orange.

White Russian - A favorite for me, it's is a simple drink to prepare. It's made with alcohol, coffeeliqueur, and heavy cream. It's a bit sweet.

The best spring cocktails

They are refreshing and light cocktails that are the perfect drink to enjoy during the season of spring.

Lillet Rose Spring Cocktail - With edible flower blooms the cocktail is made up of Lillet Rose, grapefruit juice and Gin.

Sorrel Lime Cooler is an extremely refreshing drink made of water, agave nectar, citrus leaves and sorrel, and seltzer.

Strawberry-Rhubarb Sangria: A sweet drink made of sugar as well as water, Rhubarb stalks citrus juice, strawberries, orange Seltzer, chilled champagne and seltzer.

Honey-Vanilla Splash - This drink is comprised of vanilla bean lemon juice, seltzer and lime juice.

Rum Punch - This can be extremely sweet and it is easy to mix. The ingredients are a light rum, pineapple juice, orange juice, lime juice Cranberry juice and grenadine. It's topped with a slice of lime.

Cocktails that are perfect for the summertime

They are great to cool off in the summer heat.

Sauternes along with Frozen Stone Fruit - A delicious drink with Apricots, peach, apricots nectar, and Sauternes.

Pineapple as well as Mango Rum Cocktails - A mix of some of my favourite fruit; it's the result of a mixture of mangoes the rum, along with pineapple juice.

Watermelon-Basil Margarita: A chilled margarita made with watermelon silver tequila, sugar basil leaves, triple sec and.

Blackberry-Mint Julep is a Slush with milled leaves, blackberries sugar, bourbon, and some sprigs.

Tequila Sunrise - An all-time favourite cocktail which blends the juice of an orange, tequila, and the juice of pomegranates.

Pink Salty Dog - This cocktail's name is intriguing to me. The ingredients are salt, grapefruit slice vodka and grapefruit juice. Campari Liquor.

Chapter 24: Easy Clean Up After The Party

The party you host at home will not stop when guests have left. It is finished when you've cleaned up the mess as well as removed decorations. set the furniture back the place it was before, cleaned all dishes, and then put any leftovers into the refrigerator. It sounds like a lot of task. However, we are able to simplify the process with a simple procedure.

You don't have to spend endless hours cleaning when your guests are gone. It's tiring to complete all the cleaning, arranging and tidying. It is tiring not to mention it is also the most boring. But, it is possible to use intelligent planning and organization to reduce your cleaning time by less than a quarter.

If you ever organize a party, think about these suggestions to cut down on cleaning up after the event:

Trash Bins

Set up trash bins throughout the areas to be used at the celebration. Place them in a place that guests are likely to not be able to miss they are. However they should not hamper the movement of your guests. If you are hosting an informal event or kids' celebration, notify guests of where the garbage bins are situated to ensure that they are in a position to dispose of garbage correctly.

Cleaning Stuff

Make sure that all cleaning tools are in reach. The spilled juice on your carpet, the crumbs that are in the dirt, tissue paper under the table and, worst of all, a damaged bottle or glass are not a possibility. There'll be trash and it is possible to find litter which could damage upholstery. Keep cleaning supplies in a place where it isn't necessary to take the time searching for it should you have to get rid of the stain.

Disposables

If you are able hiring a caterer that is, you will not have be concerned about washing dishes. But if have a budget that is tight and still want to host an incredible party, while cutting off on the work you do by purchasing disposable plates including cups and plates. It is easy to dispose of them when you're done, meaning that you will have less to wash following the event!

Leftovers

In the end, you must take care of the food leftovers. It is up to you to determine if the food remains acceptable for consumption or must be destroyed. In order to avoid throwing away any additional food items, you could invite your guests to bring with them some leftovers. But, of course, you could only do that if are intimately acquainted with your guests and maintain a close rapport with the guests. If you are able to this, it's an excellent method to make use of leftovers.

Chapter 25: Party Ideas

1. Roaring twenties party! Celebrities, champagne, dancing and jazz music what a fun time that must have been! Maybe, your bride and groom have this theme already within their wedding what a neat way to correlate the two. Have all the girls dress like flappers or any nineteen twenties attire. Deck your bride out with long pearls, a headband, and feathers! This would be a great idea just to dress up and go around town. Or you could book a location and turn it into your own speakeasy. Another idea to go along with this would be to hire a dancer to teach everyone how to burlesque dance.

2. Ugly dress party! This a sure way to get noticed! Go to the thrift store and purchase an old wedding dress for the bride. All the bridesmaids could either wear old wedding dresses as well or old ugly bridesmaid dresses. Go out on the town or have a fun night in taking silly recreated wedding pictures!

3. Spa party! You could either book a spa weekend somewhere or plan your own spa party at one of the girls houses. You could do each others nails or hire someone to come and do your nails for you. Enjoy relaxing face masks and of course supply the party with plenty of wine and champagne! If you are on a tight budget you can find a lot of face masks at low prices at makeup stores.

4. Paint Party! You could plan a paint party night. There are usually places around town that

offer these types of parties that include all the paints and canvases. Or you could plan it at a specific location and hire an artist to come to you.

5. Baking party! Either at a specific location or you could have a dessert tasting all around town at different locations. This would be a great idea for a pregnant bride or for those with a sweet tooth! Another

idea would be to make it a pie party and give each girl a different type of pie to bring. Have them bring the recipe with them and place it into a book for the bride to keep. You could also have an apron made for the bride that says something like soon to be Mrs. so and so.

6. Sexy themed party! Hire a toy expert to come to the party and have a dance teacher there to teach everyone pole dancing. Tell guests to bring lingerie as a present for the bride.

7. Country themed party! Have all the girls dress in their boots and cowgirl hats. Make a special cow girl hat for the bride. Go out on the town and go line dancing! Or plan it at a specific location and use decorations made with mason jars, hay barrels, burlap and twine. Serve things like lemonade, moonshine and apple cider.

8. Breakfast at Tiffany 's party! The era is set in the nineteen sixties it is about an

independent woman who falls in love with a lonely writer. In the movie Audrey Hepburn wears beautiful dresses and her favorite store is Tiffany's. You could go out on the town and all dress the part with the bride of course in the prettiest dress of them all. You could all wear big fake diamonds and look fabulous! You could also host the party at a private location and use the Tiffany blue color and fake diamonds for your decorations. You could serve mint juleps and whiskey on the rocks like she drinks in the movie.

9. Wine Party! Make personalized wine glasses for the bride and other bridesmaids. Have all the girls bring wine and make some cheese plates to along with the wine. You could even make personalized wine bottles. At any craft store you can purchase blank stickers that you can write on with a Sharpie or print on from your computer. All you have to do is soak a bottle of wine in cold water for a couple hours and then peel off

the label and let dry and then add your personalized sticker. Or you could all go wine tasting at a local winery.

10. Traditional bachelorette party! Traditional bachelorette parties usually consists of male strippers and anything shaped like a penis. Penis necklaces , penis blow up toys, penis cups , penis straws and anything else festively shaped like a penis. You can find everything you need for a traditional party at a local party store. The night usually starts with renting a limo or a party bus to take you around town. Start with a nice dinner and then bar hopping!

11. Movie night party! For movie buffs get all the girls together and have a love story movie night. Put together a montage of classic romantic chick flicks or any other theme you think your bride would like. Eat popcorn , drink cocktails and wine, play movie trivia games, and you could have a candy bar setup for everyone to enjoy. Another idea you could do is put together a

slide-show movie of the bride and groom and narrate their love story to view at the party. Tell the story of how they met, where they went on their first date, where their first kiss was, when and where they said I love you, and how and where he proposed.

12. Sushi party! Schedule a sushi making class or hire someone to come teach you at a set location. Serve hot or cold sake and hot tea. You could even hire a hot male model to be the centerpiece to hold the plates you will eat the sushi off of.

13. Candle making party! This is a fun craft for all the girls to do together! You can find everything you need at any local craft store.

14. Fondue Party! Serve melted cheese and chocolate with veggies, fruit, bread, and cakes for dipping. You can find lots of recipes online. All you need is a portable burner, a double broiler fondue pot, and fondue skewers!

15. Karaoke Party! Go out on the town or hire a karaoke DJ to come to a private location. If you want to make it really fun you could all dress like famous singers like Cher, Madonna, Britney Spears, Miley Cyrus or Lady Gaga! Play a game to see how many people ask for your autograph.

16. Luau Party! If you can't take the bride to Hawaii then bring Hawaii to her! Everyone dress in grass skirts or funny floral shirts. Make sure you all get laid with flowers that is! You could go out on the town like this it would be hilarious or have a private party on the beach or pool side. Serve drinks like pina coladas in hollowed out coconuts or pineapples. Serve tuna poke(you can find recipes online) and roast pork for dinner . Hire male dancers to do the hulaing or hire a dance instructor to teach you girls how to hula.

Getaways

When looking for the best deals on hotels, flights, cabin rentals, cruises and car rentals I always look online at places like Expedia.com, Hotwire.com, and Kayak.com

1. Vegas! Las Vegas, Nevada the ultimate sinful party destination. You girls can get into a lot of trouble here! There is so much to do from casinos, shows, shopping, and of course strip clubs!

2. Take a cruise! Enjoy fun in the sun, gambling, shows, delicious food and drinks, and shopping in the ports of call. The Bahamas, Mexico,Hawaii ,Jamaica or anywhere in the Caribbean are all really fun locations! Plus you can usually find pretty good deals and food is included with the price. Carnival Cruise.com, Norwegian Cruise.com, Princess Cruise.com

3. Book an all inclusive resort! Choice a tropical destination like the Dominican Republic, Jamaica, Mexico or Hawaii. This is a great idea because it is one price that the

girls can commit to early and not have to worry about prices once they get there. CheapCaribbean.com

4. Visit Savannah, Georgia! This historical city dates back to 1733 there are so many neat old buildings to explore and plenty of shops to visit during the day. At night you can stroll down to the river for a nice dinner and drinks. Also, its only a thirty minute drive to the beach on Tybee Island or you can head a little further to Hilton Head Island.

5. Book a weekend at a ski resort ! Theses are some great locations Colorado at Breckenridge, Copper Mountain or Steamboat, in Utah at Deer Valley, or in California at North star-at-Tahoe. Sip hot cocoa while you dine in a fancy restaurant on top of a mountain lodge or go on a distillery tour and learn about historic saloons. Have a relaxing massage in the spa after a long day on the slopes or unwind in an indoor hot tub.

6. South Beach! Miami, Florida. Have fun in the sun, people watch(you may even spot a few celebrities) .Walk down Ocean Drive for some awesome shopping, clubs, bars, and amazing restaurants.

7. Visit Key West, Florida! Known for its beautiful beaches, shopping, and nightlife on Duval street. Relax on the beach, rent bikes or mop heads,take a sunset cruise, go snorkeling, rent jet skis, travel to the most southern point or visit a spa. There are many delicious restaurants to dine at with the freshest seafood straight from the Ocean. Head to Mallory Square to watch the street performers with a beautiful sunset view! There are also non traditional attractions including clothing optional hotels and bars.

8. Napa Valley, California .Book a weekend of relaxation and wine tastings at local wineries. The countryside is beautiful and there are over 300 wineries!

9. Visit New Orleans, Louisiana! This historical port founded in 1718 is well known for it's nightlife on Bourbon street. Not only is there plenty of nightlife there are many historical places and other exciting places to check out including a zoo, aquarium, and botanical gardens.

10. Road Trip! Rent an RV and head wherever you girls want to go making fun stops along the way! Cruise America.com

11. Rent a cabin in the woods! Enjoy mountain views, go hiking, visit caves or waterfalls, tell ghost stories and roast marshmallows! You could bring stuff to do facials and paint each others nails. And if there is a TV in the cabin make sure to bring some chick flicks! VRBO®.com, FlipKey.com

Chapter 26: Games

Here are a list of game ideas for the bride to do as well as other games for everyone else to play. These can also be used as a way to break the ice and help everyone get to know each other.

1. Scavenger hunt

This game is for the bride but she can also ask the girls for help too. The goal of this game is for the bride to collect certain items and do silly tricks to guys throughout the night. The bride may tell the guy he has just been apart of the game after she has completed the task.

Examples:

Collect three separate guys phone numbers.

Get a kiss on the cheek from a blonde, brunette, silver fox, and a redhead.

Ask a guy to pretend he is your groom and practice walking down the aisle.

Go up to any guy and ask him to give you his boxers.

Ask a guy to buy you a shot: But you must insist it be a redheaded slut, a blow-job shot, a blue balls shot, an angels tit shot, a sex with an alligator shot, an anus burner shot, a liquid Viagra shot, the leg spreader shot, or an ass shot.

Go up to a guy and tell him you peed your pants and then run away.

Collect as many business cards as possible. But you must say "hey I'm in the business of bullshit marketing can I have your business card? "

Ask anyone in the bar if you can give them a spanking.

Ask a guy if you can borrow a condom because you accidentally flushed your last one down the toilet.

Dance with the nerdiest looking guy in the bar.(But don't make him feel nerdy).

Ask a bald man if you can kiss the top of his head.

Ask a guy to do the hokey pokey with you. You put your left hand in, you put your left hand out, put your left hand in then you shake it all about, you do the hokey pokey and you turn yourself around that's what its all about! Clap Clap

Start a conversation with a guy and then start repeating everything he says.

Ask a guy to sing you your favorite song or any funny song you can think of.

Tell a guy that you would love to meet his mom so you can introduce her to your dad.

See how many times you can slip in the word "meow" while talking to a guy. " Well meow long have you been a real estate attorney? How meowny times have you been to this place before?" End the conversation with " I am a crazy cat lady meow and walk away."

Ask a guy if you can buy him a drink. If he says yes order him a really girly drink like a cosmopolitan or a lemon drop martini.

2. Crossword Puzzle

Write out your own crossword puzzle use words that pertain to the couple or words that pertain to weddings or proposals.

Word Examples: Wedding, Bride, Groom, Diamond, Ring,Their names, Wedding location,His last name.

3. Romantic Movie Test

For this test use questions about famous love story movies like Pretty Woman or The Notebook.

Examples:

Question: What are the main characters names in the Notebook?

Answer: Noah Calhoun and Allison Nelson

Question: What movie features a hooker and a businessman falling in love?

Answer: Pretty Woman

Question: What year was Gone With the Wind released?

Answer: 1939

Question: Is Ashley a male or female in the movie Gone With the Wind?

Answer: Male

Question: Where is the plot set in the movie Love Actually? Starring Hugh Grant, Liam Neeson, and Martine McCutcheon.

Answer: London, England

Question: What war is depicted in the classic 1943 movie Casablanca?

Answer: World War II

Question: What is the main character Frances' nickname in the movie Dirty Dancing?

Answer: Baby

Question: In the movie The Proposal Sandra Bullock's character must marry Ryan Reynolds' character in order to avoid deportation back to which country?

Answer: Canada

Question: In the movie the Titanic what is Rose's Fiances name?

Answer: Cal

Question: In the movie When Harry Met Sally on what holiday do they finally claim their love for one another?

Answer: New Years Eve

Question: In the movie Dear John what do John and Savannah always say to each other when they part?

Answer: "I'll see you soon, then."

Question: In the movie Forgetting Sarah Marshall what the main character Peter Bretter's occupation?

Answer: A music composer for a TV

Question: In the movie The Wedding Singer Robbie (Adam Sandler) sings what song to Julia (Drew Barrymore) on the airplane?

Answer: Grow Old With You

Question: What are the main characters name in the movie Pretty in Pink?

Answer: Andie Walsh and Blane McDonough

Question: In the movie Just married Tom and Sarah's honeymoon is ruined when Sarah's ex boyfriend who shows up?

Answer: Peter

Question: In the movie My Best Friend's Wedding Julianne Potter (Julia Roberts) and Michael O' Neal (Dermot Mulroney) made a pact in college that if they were not married by what age then they would marry each other?

Answer: 28

Question: In the movie Never Been Kissed the main character Josie (Drew Barrymore) waits for her crush Sam (Michael Vartan) to give her her first kiss on what type of sports field?

Answer: Baseball field

Question: In the movie 50 First Dates is set in what tropical location?

Answer: Hawaii

Question: In the movie How to Lose a Guy in 10 Days the main character Andie Anderson (Kate Hudson) works for what magazine?

Answer: The Composure

Question: In the movie 27 Dresses what did Jane Nichols (Katherine Heigl) leave in the cab that Kevin Doyle (James Marsden) picked up and used to further his career?

Answer: Her day planner

Question: In the movie Sweet Home Alabama young Melanie Smooter (Reese Witherspoon) ran away to what city after marrying Jake Perry (Josh Lucas)?

Answer: New York City

Question: In the movie You've Got Mail what are the main characters Kathleen Kelly (Meg Ryan) and Joe Fox's (Tom Hanks) screen names?

Answer: "Shopgirl" and "NY152"

Question:The movie Valentine's Day was released in February of what year?

Answer: 2010

Question: The movie Reality Bites is set in what state?

Answer: Houston. Texas

Question: Who were the main characters Cameron James and Kat Stratford played by in the movie 10 Things I Hate About You?

Answer: Joseph Gordon-Levitt and Julia Stiles

4. Questions About the Bride and Groom

Have everyone take this test. The bride included because her test will be the answer sheet.

Examples:

Where was their first date?

Who asked who out?

How did they meet?

Where did he propose?

What is the groom's middle name?

Who are the grooms best men?

Where are they going on their honeymoon?

How long did it take before the bride knew he was the one?

What size ring does the bride wear?

How long did they date before he proposed ?

5. Hula Hoop Challenge

Once everyone has had a few drinks bust out some hula hoops and have contests.

Examples:

One girl versus another who can hula hoop the longest? Or time each girl individually.

Or make them sing a song while they hula hoop.

Who can come up with the best hula hoop dance routine?

How many hula hoops can you hula at one time?

6. Name That Song

Put together a collection of love songs, fun girl songs, or the bride's wedding songs. You can make it a written test or play sections of the song for the girls and have them write the name and artist of the song down.

Examples:

Girl Power Songs:

Question: Who sings Girls Just Want to Have Fun?

Answer: Cyndi Lauper

Question: Who sings Man I Feel Like a Woman?

Answer: Shania Twain

Question: Who sings Guys Do It All the Time?

Answer: Mindy McCready

Question: Who sings This One's For the Girls?

Answer: Martina McBride

Question: Who sings I'm every woman?

Answer: Whitney Houston

Question: Who sings Firework?

Answer: Katy Perry

Question: Who sings Born this Way?

Answer: Lady Gaga

Question: Who sings All I want to Do is Have Some Fun?

Answer: Sheryl Crow

Question: Who sings My Boyfriend's Back?

Answer: Angels

Question: Who sings Big Girls Don't Cry?

Answer: The Four Seasons

Love Songs:

Question: Who sings Have I Told You Lately That I love You?

Answer: Van Morrison

Question: Who sings A Man and a Woman?

Answer: Anita Kerr Singers

Question: Who sings At Last?

Answer: Etta James

Question: Who sings Sexual Healing?

Answer: Marvin Gaye

Question: Who sings Saving All My Love for You?

Answer: Whitney Houston

Question: Who sings Crazy for You?

Answer: Madonna

Question: Who sings Lets Get It On?

Answer: Marvin Gaye

Question: Who sings Strangers in the Night?

Answer: Frank Sinatra

Question: Who sings My Guy?

Answer: Mary Wells

Question: Who sings I Just Called to Say I Love You?

Answer: Stevie Wonder.

7. How Well Does the Bride Know the Groom

This one's for the bride use the same questions from # 4 Questions about the Bride and Groom. You will video record the groom while asking him theses questions prior to the bachelorette party. At the party you will then ask the same questions to the bride and play back his answers. Every question she gets wrong you will place a piece of bubble gum in her mouth and of course video tape her as well.

8. Personalized Mad Libs

Remember these fun little play on word games from when you were little? Make your own fill in the blank personalized story for your bride to be. The guests will fill in the blanks with adjectives,adverbs,nouns,colors,and numbers to create a funny story about your bride and groom. You can find examples on madglibs.com

Gifts and Extras

1. Make personalized tee shirts, bags, glasses and mugs for the bride. You can purchase everything you need at a local craft store or you can order them online. They can say things like; He Put a Ring On It, Soon to Be Mrs. So and So, I Fell and He Caught Me (put some angel wings on it and an engagement ring as the halo), I Am In Love With Mr. So and So, Off the Market, Groom's Name + Bride's Name = Love.

2. Write a fun song for the bride about your friendship and have all the girls sing it to her!

3. Put together a scrapbook for the bride. Each girl gets a certain amount of pages to fill with pictures of them together and fun memories. You can find places online that will print them for you this will make it easier for girls that don't live in the same place.

4. Put together a slide show of the bride and all her friends.

5. Make a signature cocktail for the bride and name it after her. You could use juice to make it one of her wedding colors or add food coloring to it. You could also make her a personalized cup to drink it out of.

6. Make a calendar of memories for the bride. She will be reminded for the rest of the year of how much she is loved by all of her friends.

7. Make a poster with the bride and grooms astrological signs on it and reasons why they are a compatible match. You can find a lot of information online about astrological signs and compatibility. You could even hire a fortune teller to come to the party as well.

8. Pick out love stories from the Bible and put them into a scrapbook with Bible verses and pictures of the bride and groom . Example: The fruit of the spirit is love, joy, peace, patience, kindness, goodness, faithfulness, gentleness and self control. Galatians 5:22-23

9. Here is a list of some all time favorite love stories and chick flick movies.

The Notebook, Pretty Woman, Gone With the Wind , Love Actually, Casablanca, Dirty Dancing, The Proposal, BrokeBack Mountain, Titanic, When Harry Met Sally, Dear John, Forgetting Sarah Marshall, The Wedding Singer, Pretty in Pink, Just married, Friends With Benefits, Never Been Kissed,

50 First Dates, The Wedding Planner, How to Lose a Guy in 10 Days, The Last Song, 27 Dresses, Sweet Home Alabama, You've Got Mail, Valentine's Day, She's All That, Reality Bites,10 Things I Hate About You, Message in a Bottle, BreakFast at Tiffanys, Brides Maides, Jerry Maguire, Sixteen Candels, Working Girl, Clueless, Party Girl, Mystic Pizza, Notting Hil,

Father of the Bride, It's Complicated, Pride and Prejudice, Something's Gotta Give, Fried Green Tomatoes, Steel Magnolias, Legally Blonde, Thelma and Loise, Sex and the City:The Movie, Under the Tuscan Sun, Sleepless in Seattle, Little Woman, The English Patient, Two Weeks Notice, Moulin Rouge.

www.ingramcontent.com/pod-product-compliance
Lightning Source LLC
Chambersburg PA
CBHW071445080526
44587CB00014B/2003